Bobby Owsinski's

DECONSTRUCTED HITS

MODERN POP & HIP-HOP

Bobby Owsinski's

DECONSTRUCTED HITS

MODERN POP & HIP-HOP

Uncover the stories & techniques behind 20 iconic songs

Alfred Music
LEARN · TEACH · PLAY

LOS ANGELES

Alfred Music
P.O. Box 10003
Van Nuys, CA 91410-0003
alfred.com

Produced in association with Lawson Music Media, Inc.
Library of Congress Control Number: 2013951015

ISBN-10: 0-7390-7343-5
ISBN-13: 978-0-7390-7343-8

Cover illustration: record: © Dreamstime.com / Aureiko

Alfred Cares. Contents printed on 100% recycled paper.

Contents

The Hits

Preface

Of all the regular posts on my Big Picture music production blog (bobbyowsinski.blogspot.com), the most popular are always the ones involving the analysis of hit songs.

I first started doing these analyses after finding a few isolated tracks from various hits (which almost everyone loves to hear) on YouTube and providing some commentary on them. Slowly that turned into a much deeper analysis, similar to those I've included in a couple of my books to illustrate how an arrangement in a hit song actually works. Eventually I expanded on that idea to encompass a lot more than the arrangement, and that's what you'll read here. Now, each song analysis looks at the song itself (its form and lyrics), the arrangement, the sound, and its production, as well as some key song facts and trivia.

While you're reading these analyses, try listening to each song, and I guarantee you'll begin to hear it differently than ever before. You'll find yourself listening *through* the song instead of to it. Rather than the wash of a complete mix, you'll begin to hear all of the individual parts of the arrangement, the production tricks, and the audio intricacies. Most of all, my aim is to identify and highlight the tangible reasons for why the song was not only a hit, but also an enduring one. Every hit has an intangible factor to it that can't be described, but there's a lot under the hood that absolutely can.

I hope you'll enjoy reading these song analyses as much as I did making them. They are a great learning tool for any engineer, producer, songwriter, or musician, as they really do help you to look deep inside the actual workings of a hit. If you're just a fan, you'll enjoy them too, because you'll listen to some of your favorite songs in a completely new and different way.

How to Listen

Since you're reading a book about listening to music (actually *through* the music), it's helpful to have a few pointers on what to listen for. Here I break it down to a general listening technique and then add an additional advanced listening technique for musicians and engineers, who probably already have more refined listening skills. If you aren't familiar with a term, check out its meaning in the glossary at the end of the book.

General Listening Technique

While this might seem like a long list, these are just some of the things that an experienced studio ear will hear almost automatically. You can train yourself to do the same pretty easily. Just start with a few at a time, and before you know it, you'll naturally be listening *through* the song, instead of just hearing it. Beware that after listening like this, you can sometimes get too analytical and lose the enjoyment of the song for a while (it happens to most first-year college music and audio students).

- **Listen for the instruments that are providing the pulse to the song.** All music, even dreamlike ambient music, has a pulse, and that's the first thing you want to notice.
- **Listen to the ambience.** Does a vocal or an instrument sound like it's in the room right in front of you, or in a club, a church, or a cave? Is there an audible reverb tail? Can you hear it repeat after it stops playing?
- **Listen to the clarity of the mix.** Can you hear each instrument and vocal clearly in the mix? Are some buried so you can't distinguish what they are? Can you identify all the instruments that you're hearing?
- **Listen to the clarity of each instrument or vocal.** Does it sound lifelike or distorted? Is there an effect used to alter its sound?

- **Try to identify each section of the song.** Is something new happening the second and third time you hear a section? Is there a new vocal or instrument introduced? Is one taken away? Is an effect added or subtracted?
- **Try to identify the loudest thing in the mix.** Is the vocal louder than the other instruments or is it lower than the rest of the band? Is the bass out in front of the drums?
- **Identify the hook of the song.** What instrument or vocal plays it? When does it occur? Is it built around a lyric? Does it even have one?
- **Listen to the stereo soundfield of the song.** Are there instruments or vocals that only appear on one side? Are there instruments that appear on both sides?
- **Listen to the overall timbre of the song.** Does it seem bright? Too much bass? Is there an instrument or vocal that stands out because of its timbre?
- **Listen to the dynamics of the song.** Does it breath volume-wise with the song's pulse? Does it sound lifeless or do the instruments and vocals sound natural like you'd hear in a club?
- **Is the song fun to listen to?** Why? Why not?

Advanced Listening Technique

The following guidelines are for those readers who have some musical or studio knowledge, who may want to listen with a bit more precision.

- **Listen for the time signature.** Where's the downbeat and how many beats until the next one?
- **Listen for the number of different sections in the song.** Do the sections repeat? Does the song have a bridge? Is there an interlude between sections?

- **Listen for the number of bars in each section.** How long is each section? Is it the same length the next time it repeats? Are there any extra bars of music? All music isn't symmetrical in that it won't necessarily have 4-, 8-, 12-, or 16-bar sections, and in many cases you'll find an extra bar before or after a section.
- **Listen to the chord pattern(s) of the song.** Does it change from the verse to the chorus or bridge? Does it change the next time the section repeats? Is there a key change in the song?
- **Listen to the song's melody.** Are there big jumps, and if so, in what section are they?
- **Listen for any delays on individual instruments.** Is the delay timed to the track so the repeats are in sync with the pulse of the song? Is the same delay used on multiple instruments or are there different ones?
- **Listen to the ambience of the song.** Is there more than one environment? Does each one have the same decay? Does each one have the same timbre?
- **Listen for the compression in the song.** Can you identify which instruments are compressed? Can you hear the compressor working? Does the song sound more or less compressed than other songs you're familiar with?
- **Are there any doubled instruments or vocals?** Are they panned in stereo?

There are a number of other listening details besides these, but these are good starting points. Of course, the song analysis will point most of them out with more precision as you read and listen along. Happy listening!

Characteristics of the Average Hit Song

Here are some interesting characteristics common to hit songs including those in this book. You won't find them all in every song, but the majority of hit songs exhibit at least some of these traits.

- **Most hit songs have a short intro.** It's always been about getting to the point, and that never seems to change.
- **The melody in the chorus tends to be higher in pitch than the verses.** This builds intensity and energy as the song progresses.
- **The chorus and the bridge have more intensity than the verse.** This is due to either more instruments or vocals entering, or greater performance intensity from the players.
- **The song's intensity builds from beginning to end.** Most songs start off less intense, and then gradually grow with each section. It then peaks towards the end of the song, either on the bridge or the outro choruses.
- **The ending can date a song.** Songs before 2000 tended to use fade endings, but more recent songs tend to use a hard ending. Hard endings are said to play better in the digital world, where a fade is more likely to make the listener skip on to the next song.

As you go through the songs in the book you'll see a number of similarities in song form, arrangement, and production. That will be a great help if you're a songwriter, arranger, or producer. The more you know about how hits are made, the more likely you'll actually have one.

Keep in mind that even though you may not like a song or an artist, it's still worth checking out the song analysis. Hits are hits for a reason, and they are definitely hard to come by. Every song included here has some sort of magic as well as some common elements, so something can be learned from every single one.

The Five Elements of a Great Arrangement

Before we look at the first song, here's an overview of the five elements of a great arrangement, which is something you'll see in every song analysis.

Most well-conceived arrangements are limited in the number of arrangement elements that occur at the same time. An element can be a single instrument such as a lead guitar or a vocal, or it can be a group of instruments such as the bass and drums, a doubled guitar line, a group of backing vocals, and so on. Generally, a group of instruments playing exactly the same rhythm is considered an element. Examples include a doubled lead guitar or doubled vocal, both single elements even though there are two of them; also a lead vocal with two additional harmonies. Two lead guitars playing different parts can be two elements, however. A lead and a rhythm guitar can be two separate elements as well.

The five main arrangement elements are:

- **The Foundation (the rhythm section)**: The foundation is usually the bass and drums, but can also include a rhythm guitar and/or keyboards if they're playing the same rhythmic figure as the rhythm section. Occasionally, as in the case of power trios, the foundation element will only consist of drums since the bass will usually have to play a different rhythm figure to fill out the sound, so it becomes its own element.
- **The Pad:** A pad is a long sustaining note or chord. In the days before synthesizers, a Hammond Organ provided the best pad and was joined later by the Fender Rhodes. Synthesizers now provide the majority of pads but real strings or a guitar power chord can also suffice.
- **The Rhythm:** Rhythm is any instrument that plays counter to the foundation element. This can be a double-time shaker or tambourine, a rhythm guitar strumming on the backbeat, or congas

playing a Latin feel. The rhythm element is used to add motion and excitement to the track.

- **The Lead:** A lead vocal, lead instrument, or solo.
- **The Fills:** Fills generally occur in the spaces between lead lines, or they can be signature hook lines. You can think of a fill element as an answer to the lead.

Most arrangements have these five elements, but very rarely are they all present at the same time. Sometimes as few as three occur simultaneously, but any more than five elements at the same time is confusing to the listener, and usually causes listener fatigue as a result.

Take note that none of the hit songs in this book have more than five elements happening at once, which is your first lesson in creating a hit.

The Hit Song Secret

A movie director once told me, "If you can get the viewer to laugh just once and cry just once in a movie, you'll have a hit." It seems like there's an analogy to that in the record business as well, as indicated 20 years ago by British psychologist John Sloboda and verified in 2007 by John Guhn of the University of British Columbia.

Sloboda conducted an experiment in which he asked listeners to identify passages in a song that register a strong emotion such as tears or goose bumps. The listeners found 20 such passages which Sloboda then analyzed; he found that 18 contained a writing device known as *appoggiatura*. An appoggiatura can be a passing note that clashes with the melody just enough to create a temporary dissonance, an entrance of a new voice, or song dynamics, all of which create tension for the listener.

All art is based around tension and release. In painting, it's black against white. In photography, it's light against the shadows. In music, it's dissonance against harmony or quiet against loud. Tension and release makes things interesting. You can't have any kind of art without it.

When several appoggiaturas happen close to one another in a melody, it develops a constant state of tension and release, which makes the melody of a song more powerful and provokes an even stronger reaction from the listener.

It turns out that there is actually a formula for appoggiatura that's comprised of four elements:

- Passages that go from quiet to loud
- An entrance of a new instrument or harmony
- A melody that suddenly expands its range
- Unexpected deviations of melody or harmony

All of these are great songwriting and arrangement devices that I'll point out in the upcoming song analyses. The fact that there have been actual studies that verify what we intuitively know shows that there may be some validity to the fact that there's a sort of formula to making hits, even though it's usually not something the songwriter consciously thinks about. One thing's for sure: surprises in volume level, melody, and harmony are what makes a listener's spine tingle. The next time you listen to a song, be on the lookout for one.

Christina Aguilera

Beautiful

Song Facts

Album: *Stripped*

Writer: Linda Perry

Producer: Linda Perry

Studio: The Enterprise Studios (Burbank, CA)

Release Date: November 16, 2002

Length: 3:59

Sales: 1+ million worldwide

Highest Chart Position: #2 U.S. *Billboard* Hot 100, #1 U.K. Singles Chart, #1 in Argentina, Australia, Canada, Ireland, and New Zealand

"Beautiful" is the second single from Christina Aguilera's fourth studio album, *Stripped.* It's generally considered one of the strongest singles of her career and won her a Grammy award for Best Female Pop Vocal Performance as well as a nomination for Song of the Year.

The song was written by producer Linda Perry, who was planning to keep "Beautiful" for her own solo album. After hearing the song, Aguilera lobbied hard for it, and Perry only relented after hearing Christina's version of the vocal with Perry playing piano. This demo version of the song was recorded in one take to 16-track tape, with Perry playing all the instruments except for drums, organ, and Mellotron, which were overdubbed later. "Beautiful" went on to become one of the most-played songs of the decade, with an estimated six billion audience impressions.

The Song

The song form for "Beautiful" is about as simple as a pop song can have, but that's also one of its attractions. The essence of the song is a simple idea, so anything more complex just wouldn't fit in context. The song's form looks like this.

intro | verse | chorus | intro | verse |
chorus | bridge | chorus | outro

The melody of the song is very strong—especially the hook in the chorus ("You are beautiful")—and although Aguilera is capable of vocal gymnastics (you hear them on the bridge), she honors the melody by staying close to it throughout. The heartfelt lyrics reflect songwriter/producer Linda Perry's strong sexual convictions; not overly crafted as with many pop songs, they tell a story without ever feeling forced.

The BPM of the song is 78.

The Arrangement

The arrangement doesn't have a lot of layers, but what's there fills up the mix quite nicely. The intro begins with a bass slide into the piano, which plays the verse melody along with low and high string pads. When the verse begins, the lead vocal enters and the strings exit. That instrumentation continues into the chorus, where the strings enter once again.

The intro then repeats, with the drums entering, high strings playing a pedal note, and mid strings playing the verse melody. The strings exit for the first half of the second verse and reenter on the second half along with an organ line, while a harmony vocal builds on the melody.

In the second chorus, the instruments continue as does the vocal harmony, but later it is doubled to make it bigger. Then, in the bridge, the bass changes to eighth notes to make the song pulse, and doubled background vocals sing the melody while the lead vocal performs fills (which is the opposite of how it's normally done).

The song then proceeds to the third chorus, which is exactly the same instrumentally as the second except for a slight variation in the lead vocal melody. The outro breaks down to vocal ad-libs with a big string melody and arrangement.

Arrangement Elements
The Foundation: Bass and drums
The Rhythm: Piano
The Pad: Strings
The Lead: Lead vocal, background vocals on bridge
The Fills: Background vocals, lead vocal on bridge

The Sound

The sound of "Beautiful" is big and open, since that's what the arrangement demands. The only noticeable ambience is the delayed reverb on the vocal, which is filtered so it blends into the track seamlessly. The lead vocal is fairly compressed, with some sibilance breaking through in a few places toward the end.

The stereo strings are panned with the high end slightly to the right and the low end slightly to the left, and the stereo piano is panned lightly across the middle. The piano is very compressed so that whenever it's hit hard, it stays under control but the sound changes slightly. The drums are natural-sounding and very present, laying into the mix in just the right amount.

Listen Up

To the click-track leakage in the vocal hole at 3:49.

To the whisper at the beginning of the song.

To the lead vocal melody that changes slightly in the third chorus.

To how behind the beat the drum fill is going into the second verse.

The Production

Linda Perry is a great producer and there's a lot to like about her work on "Beautiful." Her first task was to keep Christina Aguilera's voice under control. Christina has a formidable talent and she's not afraid to use it; she's capable of the type of vocal gymnastics that can destroy a melody or hook. The beauty here is that she's allowed to display her talent, but only on the bridge, where she brings the song to a ringing peak. The genius of the production is that the background vocals sing the melody, allowing Christina to ad-lib without getting in the melody's way.

Another thing to listen for is the drum track played by Brian MacLeod, which was completed in a single take. Listen to how he plays behind the beat, giving the song a deep groove. You can especially hear this on his fill going into the second verse.

Lady Gaga

Born This Way

Song Facts

Album: *Born This Way*

Writers: Stefani Germanotta, Fernando Garibay, Jeppe Laursen, Paul Blair

Producers: Gaga, Fernando Garibay, Jeppe Laursen, DJ White Shadow

Studios: Abbey Road Studios (London), Germano Studios (New York City)

Release Date: May 23, 2011

Length: 4:20

Sales: 8.2 million

Highest Chart Position: #1 U.S. Billboard Hot 100 as well as 21 other countries

Whether you love Lady Gaga or hate her, her song "Born This Way" was a huge hit. It's the title track from the album of the same name, which was Gaga's second studio album that sold over a million in its first week in the U.S. alone. The song "Born This Way" went on to become one of the best selling singles ever, with over 8 million units sold.

Gaga herself played a big hand in this album, cowriting and coproducing all the songs while she was on tour, hence the songs were recorded and mixed with a variety of coproducers and cowriters all over the world. The song reached #1 in 19 countries and was the fastest selling song in iTunes history, selling over a million in five days.

The Song

"Born This Way" is a straight-down-the-middle electropop dance song that follows a familiar form. The form goes like this:

spoken intro | music intro | verse | chorus | spoken interlude | verse | chorus | bridge | chorus | chorus | spoken outro

About the only thing that's different about the song form itself is the spoken parts: the intro, interlude, and outro. That said, the song does have a good melody and a strong chorus, in the tradition of all great pop songs. Perhaps the greatest trait of the song is the lyrics, which speak to personal empowerment (there's that theme again), although the rhymes seem really forced.

The BPM of the song is 126.

The Arrangement

The song begins with a low synth arpeggio, synth and percussion sound effects and Gaga's spoken word. This leads into a musical intro with kick drum, bass and a woodblock-like percussion playing a pattern for the rhythm.

The first verse has a smaller sounding kick drum, a synth pad and the vocal, but on bar 5 the wood block percussion reenters. On bar 9 (or halfway through the first verse), the bigger sounding kick drum returns and a vocal harmony enters. On the chorus, the wood block percussion mutes and is replaced by white noise percussion, while multiple high and low harmony vocals enter, but they're spread slightly left and right in the mix while the lead vocal remains in the center.

After the chorus, a spoken word interlude enters that's half as long as the one in the intro, but has the same instrumentation. The first 4 bars of the second verse is paired down to only Gaga's lead vocal with

Photo: Paige K. Parsons/atlasicons.com

the small kick sound, but on bar 5 the bass and percussion reenter. This continues through the verse, with the only changes being the vocal ad lib at the end of bar 12 and the stop time for the last 6 beats of the verse.

The second chorus is virtually the same as the first, and is followed by a bridge that uses the same instrumentation as the original instrumental intro, with a spoken verse over the top. Halfway through the bass and pad of the chorus enter.

The next chorus differs from the previous ones in that it begins without the bass. In the next chorus, the bass reenters and only changes with Gaga's vocal ad libs. Another chorus enters without the bass and drums, with claps on 2 and 4, then yet another chorus breaks down even further without the synth pads in which the vocal melody and backgrounds changes. The song ends with synth pad playing different chords underneath another spoken-word verse.

Arrangement Elements
The Foundation: Bass, drums
The Rhythm: Aggressive synth with a sawtooth wave shape predominantly in the second half of the first verse
The Pad: Like most dance songs, a synth pad, predominantly in the first verse, but also adding glue throughout the song
The Lead: Gaga's vocal
The Fills: Something in almost every space where there's not a vocal, usually a synth or sound effects

The Sound

Once again, like most dance-oriented songs, "Born This Way" is compressed pretty hard, but the kick and snare are really squeezed to the point where they don't sound natural at all. Maybe that was the point, but the song might have sounded better with more dynamics and different samples.

Many of the sounds on this recording are somewhat distorted and what producers would call "trashy" sounding because of their lack of fidelity. This seems to be on purpose and does fit the song well, but can sometimes be a bit harsh on the ears. That said, there's a lot of sonic layering going on, with most elements having their own ambience, some of which is very short and roomy sounding except for the vocals.

Gaga's vocal has a short timed delay and a short reverb in the verses, then gets drier during the chorus. You can hear both the delay and reverb a lot better in the bridge, but notice how it blends into the track when more instruments and voices are added.

Listen Up

To the first half of the verse where you only hear the vocal, pad, and rhythm.

To the first four bars of the second verse where you hear just the vocal and kick drum.

To the first half of the bridge with only spoken word, synth bed, and sound effects.

To the first half of the first outro chorus with just vocals and kick drum.

To the last outchorus vocal where it breaks down to just the lead and harmony vocals.

The Production

The breakdown of the vocals in the outro chorus is one of the highlights of the song. There's some nice ad-libbing by Gaga, and the vocal harmony twists at the end are small, yet attention grabbing.

That said, this is a very thick production—there's always something going on, even if it might be subtle. New vocal parts enter when you least expect it, and there are many vocal twists. It's the kind of production you expect from an artist of this magnitude.

Carly Rae Jepsen

Call Me Maybe

Song Facts

Album: *Curiosity*

Writers: Carly Rae Jepsen, Josh Ramsay, Tavish Crowe

Producer: Josh Ramsay

Studio: The Warehouse (Vancouver)

Release Date: September 20, 2011

Length: 3:13

Sales: 9+ million

Highest Chart Position: #1 U.S. *Billboard* Hot 100, #1 in 18 other countries

Canadian singer Carly Rae Jepsen's "Call Me Maybe" hit #1 on the Ultimate Chart and made Top 5 on the *Billboard* Hot 100. The song, from her album *Curiosity,* was originally written as a folk song, but later became a pop hit thanks to producer Josh Ramsay. After both Justin Bieber and Selena Gomez tweeted about the song, it took off and became a worldwide hit, going to #1 in 11 countries.

Jepsen placed third in *Canadian Idol* season five in 2007, which led to her first album, *Tug of War,* in 2008. She's gone on to receive multiple awards and nominations, including three Juno Awards and two Grammy award nominations, and was also named by *Billboard* as 2012's Rising Star.

With worldwide sales of over 13 million copies, "Call Me Maybe" was the best-selling digital single of 2012, and is one of the best-selling digital singles and one of the best-selling singles of all time.

The Song

"Call Me Maybe" is probably one of simplest pop song forms you'll ever hear, consisting of just a verse and a chorus. There is a bridge (which unusually repeats at the end of the song), but it's really just a slight melody change with some different lyrics over the chorus. The form looks like this:

verse | chorus | verse | chorus | bridge (chorus) | interlude |
chorus | bridge (chorus)

To add more time to the song, since it's so short, each chorus is repeated with just a few of the lyrics changed. Speaking of the lyrics, they fit the song well and are written around a single sentiment that most people can relate to: giving your number to someone you're attracted to. There's not much of a story, and it almost seems like the lyric writing was rushed since it feels very incomplete, especially in the bridge.

The BPM of the song is 120.

The Arrangement

The arrangement on "Call Me Maybe" is interesting for a couple of reasons. First of all, there's really not a bass instrument that can be easily heard. The low end is supplied by what sounds like a synthesizer, although a bass could be in the mix but mixed down pretty low, or it could even be a baritone guitar. Which brings us to the second point: The main instruments (strings high and low, guitar chords, bass synth) are playing the exact same figures throughout the two sections of the song, keeping the listener waiting for the bass to break out and play a walking line or counter-figure (especially after the snare fills during the song), but it never happens.

The song starts with two bars of eighth note string hits (it almost sounds like it could be a sampled guitar), which is joined by a quarter-note kick drum (four on the floor), the lead vocal, and either a guitar or another synth playing a lower part underneath the opening strings. Halfway through the verse the hi-hat, stereo harmony vocals, and a guitar playing a lower string pedal enter.

On the chorus the vocal is doubled, a new bigger kick sound is introduced along with an exploding snare sample, and a new string line doubles with a guitar. When the chorus repeats, a second guitar enters on the right playing chords and a different guitar enters on the left playing a double-time line to add some movement to the song.

On the second verse, the hi-hat pattern is varied slightly and a soft snare enters. There's also a bass synth/baritone guitar from the chorus that continues to play. The vocal now has a harmony above it, but it's in mono instead of the spread stereo of the second half of the B sections.

The bridges are interesting in that they're basically a chorus with a different melody and a guitar counter-line.

There's a hard ending to the song but it's done fairly cleverly with a slow-down and pitch-down of the existing instruments to give the song some finality.

Arrangement Elements
The Foundation: Kick drum, exploding snare in the chorus
The Rhythm: Hi-hat and guitar in the second half of the chorus push the song the most; strings, bass synth, and guitar chords push it less
The Pad: None
The Lead: Vocals
The Fills: Guitar counter-line in the bridge

The Sound

The sound of "Call Me Maybe" is very in-your-face, especially the vocals. The only ambience is the short stereo room reverb on the strings, and a long timed delay on the fill guitar in the bridge.

As is the case with most pop songs today, this one is fairly compressed, especially the vocals. You can sometimes hear the compressor pumping on the vocal, and it sounds like there was a lot of sibilance that was attenuated with a de-esser, almost too much since you sometimes can't distinguish the s's in the song.

Listen Up

To the harmony vocals of the verse and chorus which are doubled and spread left and right.

To the mono guitars in the chorus panned to the left and right.

The Production

For a song that has just two-and-a-half sections (if you count the bridge/ chorus), it does develop pretty well dynamically speaking. If you listen closely you can hear the instruments enter and exit, especially from the beginning of the song until just after the first bridge. Sometimes it's subtle, but there's always something new happening to capture your attention.

The vocal performance by Jepsen is especially strong as it varies just enough to keep the melody from being boring, yet never sounds forced. In fact, you could say that it even carries the song, which is exactly what you want in a pop song.

Beyoncé (featuring Jay-Z)

Crazy in Love

Song Facts

Album: *Dangerously in Love*

Writers: Beyoncé Knowles, Rich Harrison, Shawn Carter, Eugene Record

Producers: Rich Harrison, Beyoncé Knowles

Studio: Sony Music Studios (New York City)

Release Date: May 18, 2003

Length: 3:56

Sales: 8+ million worldwide (single), 11+ million worldwide (album)

Highest Chart Position: #1 U.S. *Billboard* Hot 100, #1 U.K. Singles Chart

"Crazy in Love" is the first single from Beyoncé Knowles' first solo album, *Dangerously in Love*, which rocketed her to fame as a solo artist. The song hit #1 in both the U.S. and U.K. and was Top 10 around the world. It also went on to win Grammy awards for Best R&B Song and Best Rap/Sung Collaboration.

Writer/producer Rich Harrison had previously recorded a demo for the song, which was based around a horn sample from The Chi-Lites' 1970 tune "Are You My Woman (Tell Me So)". Much to his surprise, he received some resistance from Beyoncé about using the sample on the album because she thought it "too retro." Harrison wrote the verses and the hook (inspired by a saying Beyoncé had about her "crazy" appearance), while Beyoncé wrote the bridge. Late in the production, after most of the recording was already complete, Jay-Z provided the rap verse.

The Song

"Crazy in Love" is based around a couple of song samples that are turned into multiple parts, thanks to some ingenious songwriting and arrangement. The song form looks like this:

intro | interlude | intro | verse | chorus | interlude |
verse | chorus | verse (rap) | interlude (rap) |
bridge | chorus | chorus | outro

The intro, chorus, and bridge are built around one sample, while the verses are built around another—and both samples are from The Chi-Lites' 1970 song "Are You My Woman (Tell Me So)."

The lyrics aren't going to win any poetry awards and the rap seems disjointed. The hook lyrics in the chorus also seem a bit wordy and don't flow well with the music, although that may have more to do with the sample than the lyric itself.

The BPM of the song is 99.

The Arrangement

The intro consists of the main horn sample from "Are You My Women (Tell Me So)." This is accompanied by a Jay-Z rap, which proceeds to an interlude of doubled vocals over a conga sample from the same record. Another intro follows and then the verse begins, which is over the same conga sample, and is augmented with a sampled horn stab on the downbeat every 2 bars. What's interesting is that the sample seems a little short on the chorus, and this causes the vocal melody to seem like it's almost out of the pocket.

The chorus is over the main horn and rhythm section sample, with the vocals doubled the first two times through the pattern; a harmony vocal

Photo: Eddie Malluk/atlasicons.com

is added the third time through, while the tag features Beyoncé's full three-part harmony.

After the chorus, there is another interlude. This is followed by the second verse, which is essentially the same as the first, but with different fills. The second chorus is also the same except for an additional ad-libbed vocal and a tag on the end.

Jay-Z raps over the next verse and interlude, with the rap being doubled on the interlude. The bridge then occurs over the chorus sample and features rich three-part harmony that actually changes the chord structure from a minor chord to a major where the song peaks. The last two choruses are identical to the second chorus except for an additional ad-lib, while the outro is just the sample minus the vocals into a fade ending.

While the song is built around the samples, the verse sample is augmented with an additional kick drum, snare, and kick sound from a Roland TR-808 drum machine.

Arrangement Elements
The Foundation: The loop from "Are You My Women (Tell Me So)"
The Rhythm: Congas (from the sample)
The Pad: None
The Lead: Lead vocal, horn sample in the intro and chorus
The Fills: Background vocals, whistle, rap, and vocal ad-libs

The Sound

Sonically, there's not much going on in "Crazy in Love." The samples are slowed down from the original song, but they're far from what you'd call high fidelity. Most of the vocals have a modulation effect, and while the doubles are spread slightly left and right, there's not much going on in the stereo field except for a few ad-lib fills. The audio was obviously not a priority on this song, nor should it have been, since it was chiefly based on lo-fi samples in the first place.

Listen Up

To the subtle modulation on the vocals.

To the various fills throughout the verses in between the lead vocal phrases.

To the double on Jay-Z's rap vocal on the second half of the rap section.

The Production

The brilliance of the production on "Crazy in Love" is how the song was constructed around only a couple of samples. When you consider that—at its densest—the song consists of a sample and doubled background harmony vocals with an ad-lib, it would seem to take up only about 12 tracks. Considering that most modern productions may hit over a hundred tracks, that says a lot for how the song was put together. It's basic in so many ways, and that's probably why it was a big hit.

Gnarls Barkley

Crazy

Song Facts

Album: *St. Elsewhere*

Writers: Brian Burton, Thomas Callaway, Gian Franco Reverberi, Gian Piero Reverberi

Producer: Danger Mouse

Studio: Maze Studios (Atlanta, GA)

Release Date: March 23, 2006

Length: 2:58

Sales: 2+ million (single)

Highest Chart Position: #2 U.S. *Billboard* Hot 100, #1 U.K. Singles Chart, #1 European Hot 100, #1 in Austria, Hungary, Ireland, New Zealand, and Switzerland

Photo: Eddie Malluk/atlasicons.com

Gnarls Barkley is a musical collaboration between DJ/musician/producer Danger Mouse (Brian Burton) and singer/rapper Cee Lo Green (Thomas Callaway), and they hit worldwide pay dirt with "Crazy," the first single from their first album, *St. Elsewhere*. The group's name is a parody of celebrity names Prince Gnarls (Prince Charles) and Bob Gnarly (Bob Marley). The track is actually based on an Italian song called *"Nel Cimitero di Tucson* (In Tucson's Cemetery)" by composer Gian Franco Reverberi from the soundtrack of a western called *Preparati la bara!*

"Crazy" is the first single ever to reach #1 on the U.K. Singles Chart purely on download sales, since it was released a week prior to the CD single. It's also the longest-running #1 on the U.K. Official Download Chart, remaining there for 11 consecutive weeks.

The song won a Grammy award in 2007 for Best Urban/Alternative

Performance, as well as a 2006 MTV Europe Music Award for Best Song. In 2009, it was named Best Song of the Decade by *Rolling Stone* magazine and placed at #100 on its list of 500 Greatest Songs of All Time.

The Song

"Crazy" is a very simple song, with the most minimal of sections—just verse and chorus. What it does have is a very strong melody, especially in the chorus, as well as a couple of tricks in the groove to keep it interesting. The form looks like this:

verse | chorus | verse | chorus | verse | chorus | outro

Just as the song form is very non-traditional, so are the lyrics. They're almost stream of consciousness, but they make sense, tell a story, and fit the melody perfectly.

The BPM of this song is 111.

The Arrangement

Just like the song form, the arrangement of "Crazy" is pretty basic, but its simplicity is very effective.

The song begins with a four-count on the bass, drums, and guitar, then goes directly into the verse. The rhythm section is comprised of a drum machine kick and snare, with the kick rhythm doubled on bass and guitar. A tambourine supplies motion, while a bed of sampled vocals supplies the pad behind the vocal.

At the chorus, a second layer of background vocals enters an octave higher than in the verse, along with a string line that plays counter to the melody. This same verse and chorus repeats three times with one minor variation: the drums drop out of a bar in the middle of the third verse. Otherwise, the sections are identical to the first verse and chorus.

The outro is half of a verse with a vocal ad-lib over the top. The drums drop out on the last 2 bars, and the bass, drums, and vocals end on the downbeat of the next cycle of chords.

Arrangement Elements
The Foundation: Drum machine kick and snare, bass with a doubled guitar line
The Rhythm: Tambourine
The Pad: Synth playing a vocal chorus sample up to the chorus, where a second set of vocals comes in an octave higher
The Lead: Lead vocal
The Fills: String lines during chorus

THE SOUND

"Crazy" features a lead vocal with a deep timed echo for ambience that is prominently heard at the end of phrases. The rhythm section is dry and in your face, but the strings and background vocals each have a touch of ambience to set them back in the mix. The song is compressed, but not as much as pop songs can be sometimes, and this gives the sparse arrangement some space to breathe.

Listen Up

To the tambourine and how it adds motion to the song.

To how the drums drop out midway through the third chorus.

To the vocal chorus samples behind the lead vocal throughout the song.

To each chorus and how the downbeat of the music begins 1 beat early.

The Production

"Crazy" is a stripped-down song with very few layers, but the four main elements are always playing, unlike most other songs that bring in and take out elements in order to create a sense of dynamics. This song is unusual in that the bass and doubled guitar line exactly double the kick drum, especially the 32nd note pickup at the beginning of each bar 8 of the 8-bar pattern—something that gives the song a very modern feel.

Another unusual production quirk is that the downbeat of the chorus starts 1 beat early with the music, but the vocal begins where you'd expect. This is something the average listener won't necessarily notice, but it's different enough to not sound like a typical chorus. Once again, it's the nuances and small details that help make a song a hit.

Snoop Dogg (featuring Pharrell)

Drop It Like It's Hot

Song Facts

Album: *R&G (Rhythm & Gangsta): The Masterpiece*

Writers: Chad Hugo, Calvin Broadus, Pharrell Williams

Producers: The Neptunes

Release Date: September 12, 2004

Length: 4:30

Sales: 2+ million (single)

Highest Chart Position: #1 U.S. *Billboard* Hot 100, #10 U.K. Singles Chart

"Drop It Like It's Hot" was the first single from Snoop Dogg's seventh album, *R&G (Rhythm & Gangsta): The Masterpiece*. The song was produced by The Neptunes, who also co-wrote the tune with Snoop. Producer Pharrell is featured on the first verse of the song, while Snoop does the second and third.

At the 2005 Grammy awards, the song was nominated for Best Rap Song and Best Rap Performance by a Duo or Group. In 2009, it was named Rap Song of the Decade by *Billboard* magazine. It is thought that the title and hook of the song came from a Lil Wayne song of the same name.

The Song

"Drop It Like It's Hot" is a traditional hip-hop song based around the verse and chorus, with a distinct intro and outro. The form looks like this:

intro | chorus | verse | chorus | verse | chorus | verse | chorus | intro | outro

NUTTIN BUT DA DOGG IN ME!!!
BEWARE OF DOGG!!
in the L-B
D-O-double
Keep comin'
Every sing
and my homeboys do
don't love them hoe
While you muth

The outro differs from the intro only in that it's stripped of the "Snoop" sample.

The BPM of the song is 93.

The Arrangement

The arrangement for "Drop It Like It's Hot" is beautiful in its simplicity. It's based around a couple of beats and a few samples, with a single synth line that enters just before each verse.

The song begins with the main beat and lip-smack samples, along with a lengthy "Snoop" sample. At the end of the section, the synth line enters, signaling that the chorus is coming next. The chorus consists of Snoop's lead rap and doubled answers that are spread left and right. At the end of the chorus, a new beat appears, and the rap is doubled and spread left and right.

Pharrell takes the first verse, which has the same music as the intro, minus the "Snoop" sample. On bars 7 and 8, the ending chorus beat enters, and then the verse beat begins again, only to stop on bars 13 and 14—at which point, a clock ticks and a bell rings in time with the track. In bars 15 and 16, the synth line enters again to introduce the chorus.

The second and third choruses are identical to the first and sound like they were just cut and pasted. The second verse has Snoop doing the rap, where he's introduced by a single "Snoop" sample from the intro. Once again, on bars 7 and 8, the ending chorus beat enters with a stutter edit and scratches on the vocal. The verse beat begins again and stops on bars 15 and 16, where the synth line enters again to introduce chorus.

In the last verse, Snoop again handles the rap, and on bars 7 and 8, the ending chorus beat enters. On bars 13 and 14, the kick drum is muted, and once again, on bars 15 and 16, the synth line enters to introduce the chorus.

Photo: Anthony Cutajar/atlasicons.com

When the intro reappears, the "Snoop" sample is present, but the mouth-click samples are missing. The synth line enters on bars 7 and 8, and then the intro returns into a long fade—this time with the mouth-click samples present but the "Snoop" sample missing.

Arrangement Elements
The Foundation: Drum beat
The Rhythm: Mouth-click samples, swishing percussion
The Pad: None
The Lead: Lead rap
The Fills: Rap answers, synth line

The Sound

"Drop It Like It's Hot" actually sounds a lot better than many contemporary hits in that it's very clean and not too compressed. There aren't many layers, so the mix probably wasn't too complicated; and like most rap songs, everything is dry and in your face, except for a slight delay on the "Snoop" samples and synth line, which you can really hear on the outro at about 4:10.

There isn't a lot of wide panning, but things are spread across the stereo field. The swishing percussion in the background is spread slightly from left to right, and the lip-smack samples pan from left to right. Where you really hear the stereo sound, though, is on the rap answers during the chorus, as the double adds intensity and depth to the section.

Listen Up

To the stereo doubles on the rap during the chorus.

To how sometimes during the verse, everything but the vocal is muted on beat 4 of a measure.

To the bell and clock at bars 13 and 14, near the end of the first verse.

To the subtle swishing percussion in the background.

The Production

When it comes to record production, simplicity may be one of the hardest things to learn. Especially in these days of almost unlimited available tracks, it's very easy to add a lot of tracks and layers in the name of experimentation, and then want to try to use them all during the mix. The Neptunes understand simplicity though, and they're quite willing to go with a stripped-down arrangement when it works, as it does here.

As with most hits, the little things make all the difference, and "Drop It Like It's Hot" is no exception. Listen to the clock and bell, punctuating the end of the first verse. Listen to the second verse, where Snoop mentions a DJ and is answered by a stutter edit and turntable scratch. Listen to the outro, where the first 8 bars feature the "Snoop" sample with no lip smacks, and then it's turned around on the next 8 bars of the fade. These are the things that, by keeping a listener's attention, can help make a song a hit.

Katy Perry

Firework

Song Facts

Album: *Teenage Dream*

Writers: Katy Perry, Mikkel S. Eriksen, Tor Erik Hermansen, Sandy Wilhelm, Ester Dean

Producers: Stargate, Sandy Vee

Studio: Roc the Mic Studio (New York)

Release Date: October 26, 2010

Length: 3:40

Sales: 5+ million

Highest Chart Position: #1 U.S. *Billboard* Hot 100, #1 Canadian Hot 100

Katy Perry's hit "Firework" epitomizes the best of current production (done by the production team Stargate and Sandy Vee, who are also cowriters of the song). The song was the third single from her second album *Teenage Dream,* and went to #1 on the *Billboard* charts and Top 5 in 20 countries around the world. It was also the fifth most played song in the United States in 2011, according to Nielsen Broadcast Data Systems.

"Firework" was nominated for both Record of the Year and Best Solo Performance Grammys, and the video for the song won Video of the Year at the 2011 MTV Video Music Awards. The video is also the most viewed of all Perry's songs on YouTube.

Perry considers "Firework" one of her best songs because of the positive message it sends, and because so many people have embraced it to help them feel more confident about themselves.

Photo: Larry Marano/atlasicons.com

The Song

"Firework" is a more or less traditional pop song in that it has a common structure found in most hits that looks like this:

short intro | verse | B section | chorus | chorus | verse | B section | chorus | chorus | bridge | chorus | chorus | outro

That doesn't mean it's boring though. The song builds nicely and takes us through a couple of peaks (one at the bridge and one at the outro), thanks to its built-in dynamics. It even has an ending, which is becoming more the norm for a pop song, instead of the slow fade that most pop songs once had.

While it's easy to concentrate on the music of "Firework," the lyrics may be much more important to the song, at least in the view of many listeners. Katy sings of personal empowerment, a theme that resonates with young and old alike, in an elegant manner that doesn't seem at all forced. All the rhymes work where they need to, and where they don't, they still feel natural.

The BPM of the song is 124.

The Arrangement

The arrangement is state-of-the-art. The intro and first verse are very sparse, with the strings entering at the first B section and continuing to build to a crescendo through the first chorus. The chorus repeats with additional movement thanks to the entrance of the bass.

The song begins with an intro of two synths playing by themselves, one playing the eighth-note chords and the other play quarter notes but on the upbeat or "1 and, 2 and, "etc. That leads to the verse where the lead vocal enters along with the drums and claps on beat 4, although they're mixed very low. On the B section, both the synths and drums are muted in favor of the strings, which leads in to the first chorus, during which the vocals are doubled, the bass synthesizer enters, and the snare drum builds.

When the chorus repeats, the drums enter and stay in the song for the next verse. On the second verse the bass drops out and the synths reenter, but the claps are now on 2 and 4 and double the tom fills at the end of bars 4 and 8. The bass reenters for the second half of the verse. Once again at the B section, the everything mutes except for the strings and the snare build on the last 3 bars. This time both choruses have strings bass, drums and doubled vocals, but between choruses the strings and bass play a turnaround line. On the second chorus the song builds with harmony vocals with the lead vocal.

During the bridge, the bass and drums continue to play the same feel, but are joined by a low synth pad for tension. The vocals are doubled for the first half, but just a single lead vocal on the second half.

The next chorus starts with just the strings and an eighth-note low synth with the doubled vocal. A drum fill leads into the next chorus that has the bass and drums re-entering along with a harmony lead vocal. The melody is also changed slightly.

The outro has the chorus music with a variation of the bridge melody and lyrics that are sung in harmony. The song ends with a hard ending after a reprise of the same string and bass turnaround previously used in the second chorus.

Arrangement Elements
The Foundation: Bass and drums
The Rhythm: Keyboard playing eighth notes, strings
The Pad: Synth in the bridge
The Lead: Lead vocal
The Fills: Strings in the chorus

The Sound

Once again, here is an example of how the sound of pop records has returned to the 1980s and '90s in that everything except the drums has some ambience to it, which provides depth. Katy has what sounds like a timed triplet delay on her voice which triggers the reverb, so there's depth and spaciousness without washing out. The same is true on the rest of the track in that there's some space around each instrument except for the bass and drums, which are dry and in your-face.

While "Firework" isn't what we'd call "hypercompressed" where all of the excitement is squeezed out of it, it's still heavily compressed. This seems unavoidable in pop music these days, as every producer and/or label tries to make their record sound louder than the competition.

Listen Up

To the entrance of the line in-between the repeat of the second chorus.
To the harmony vocals on the repeats of the chorus.
To the background vocal answers in the outro.
To how the vocal melody subtly changes on the second and third choruses.

The Production

As mentioned, "Firework" features state-of-the-art production in all aspects. It's a well-written song, it's recorded and mixed very well, and the arrangement is top notch in that the song has a lot of dynamics that keep the song interesting and moving.

It's easy to think of Katy Perry as a lightweight because of her celebrity and exposure, but the girl has some pipes and this song proves it. She really sells the song and pulls you in. Plus, she sings harmony vocals with herself very well, which many singers can't do.

Great production is not only about getting great performances but making sure that the song is exciting. Mission accomplished.

Pink

Get the Party Started

Song Facts

Album: *Missundazstood*

Writer: Linda Perry

Producer: Linda Perry

Release Date: October 9, 2001

Length: 3:11

Sales: 12+ million worldwide (album)

Highest Chart Position: #4 U.S. *Billboard* Hot 100, #2 U.K. Singles Chart

"Get the Party Started," the first single from Pink's second album, *Missundaztood*, is the song that would restart singer/songwriter Linda Perry's career. After receiving a cold call from Pink, in which the pop star declared her admiration for 4 Non Blondes (Perry's disbanded all-female group), Perry wrote "Get the Party Started" in her bedroom, programming the entire song except for the bass and wah guitar. As she included every cliché imaginable, Perry realized the song was not only her first dance song, but also a potential hit.

"Get the Party Started" was a huge hit all over the world, and it reached #4 on the U.S. *Billboard* Hot 100 chart. The song was nominated for a Grammy award for Best Female Pop Vocal Performance, and won the award for Best Song at the MTV Europe Music Awards of 2002. The song is listed as #81 in *Rolling Stone*'s Top Songs of the 2000s.

The Song

"Get the Party Started" has a relatively simple song form. The basic

beat and chord structure remains the same throughout, while the melody and arrangement change to define the verses and choruses. The form looks like this:

intro | chorus | verse | chorus | verse | chorus |
bridge/verse | verse | chorus | chorus | outro | ending

There's a brief section before the third verse that acts as a bridge, as it provides relief from the melody and lyrics, but there are no other sections to the song.

The melody and hook, both memorable and singable, are very strong. The lyrics are simplistic, but they rhyme well and tell a story without sounding forced.

The BPM of the song is 130.

The Arrangement

Any song with a simple form or chord structure needs a sophisticated arrangement in order for the listener to want to hear it over and over again; and, indeed, that's the case with "Get the Party Started."

The song begins with a whispered vocal and what sounds like a regenerated build into the main groove, which lasts for 4 bars and then leads immediately into the chorus. The main groove is built around programmed drums, with straight eighths being played on the hi-hat. Also present is a distorted synth line and a wah guitar. The bass guitar and kick drum play the same rhythm. The intro's distorted synth line is repeated during the chorus throughout the song.

In the chorus, the vocals harmonize and then turn into a unison, double-panned left and right, with a high horn stab in the right channel and a low one in the left. In the verse, the vocal sounds smaller and moves to the middle, but synths and other vocals continually enter—not in the "holes" between phrases of the main vocal, but along with it.

Horns accompany the main vocal at the beginning of the second verse, and they also appear in the holes at the end of the second phrase. The music stops halfway through except for the lead vocal and a laugh, and then continues to the next chorus, which is the same as the previous one except for the different fills that appear again with the melody. On the second chorus, the horns get bigger and a vocal ad lib appears in the center of the stereo field.

On the bridge/verse, a new wah guitar enters, accompanied by an occasional tom fill, and plays the verse's melody; this continues to another synth build at the beginning of the next verse.

The third verse has further variation. It features a band-limited single vocal, which is a lot "smaller" than the vocal on the previous verse. Plus, there are fewer fills and less instrumentally going on underneath. A doubled vocal is used for the last two phrases, and the verse ends with a ping-pong delay.

In the last chorus, a programmed tambourine and low horns are added, and the outro starts with an ad-libbed vocal in the middle, then on the left, then right, and then back again. The song ends as it began, with a regenerated build leading into a car shifting gears and a laugh.

Arrangement Elements
The Foundation: Bass and drums
The Rhythm: Guitar with wah
The Pad: None
The Lead: Lead vocals, distorted synth in intro, guitar with wah in bridge
The Fills: Horns, synth

The Sound

"Get the Party Started" features a variety of sonic environments that act as layers. The vocal has a number of timed delays ranging from hardly audible to long single and ping-pong delays occurring only on one line. The main vocal in the verse is intentionally thin to set it off from the doubled, larger-sounding vocals of the chorus.

The drums don't especially stand out, except the sound of the kick is so big that it completely covers the bass guitar, which, for more of a dance-record sound, has little definition and is used only as support.

Most of the instruments are fairly dry and up front in the mix, but the horn stabs have a delayed reverb with a long tail, and the lead vocal has a timed delay, with brief passages of longer or even ping-pong delays at the end of the second chorus.

The panning is very balanced, with the hi-hat slightly to the right and the wah guitar to the left. The vocal on the main verse is in the center, but on the chorus, the vocals are spread out left and right.

The high horn stabs enter on the right, while the lower ones enter on the left; but in the chorus, the low horns stay in the middle. Various synths enter throughout the song in different areas of the soundfield, and all sound effects, like the car burning rubber, pan from right to left.

Listen Up

To the high horn stabs on the right, then the low ones on the left in the chorus.

To the fills in every vocal space.

To the car burning rubber, which pans right to left in the second verse.

To the ping-pong delay at the end of the third verse.

The Production

When a song is mostly programmed, the producer's job is to get the best performance possible from the vocals and whatever instruments are recorded live—and use whatever means necessary with the overdubs to keep the song interesting.

Producer Linda Perry exercises constraint on the formidable vocal chops of Pink, allowing her to use her considerable gift in places that bring the song to a new level of intensity, like during the choruses and outro. In fact, what's backward in a good way is that the song peaks on the outro instead of during a chorus or bridge like most songs. Another thing that's different from other productions is that many of the fills occur behind the vocal, instead of in the spaces between the phrases. This helps to build up the tension and release from the verse to the chorus and back again, holding the listener's interest every step of the way.

Bruno Mars
Grenade

Song Facts

Album: *Do-Wops & Hooligans*

Writers: Bruno Mars, Philip Lawrence, Ari Levine, Moe Faisal, Brody Brown, Claude Kelly, Andrew Wyatt

Producer: The Smeezingtons (Bruno Mars, Philip Lawrence, and Ari Levine)

Studio: Larrabee Recording Studios, Levcon Studios (Los Angeles)

Release Date: September 28, 2010

Length: 3:42

Sales: 7 million

Highest Chart Position: #1 U.S. Pop and *Billboard* Hot 100, #1 in Australia, Canada, Czech Republic, Denmark, Germany, Ireland, Israel, New Zealand, Norway, Poland, Scotland, Sweden, Switzerland, United Kingdom

"Grenade" was the breakout single from Bruno Mars' debut album *Do-Wops & Hooligans*, which went on to become a huge worldwide hit. Not only did the song hit #1 in 15 countries, but it also charted Top 10 in 11 others while selling seven million units. The album also went on to sell over 4 million copies, going #1 in six countries and Top 10 in 13 others. "Grenade" was nominated for Record of the Year, Song of the Year, and the Pop Solo Performance Grammys, losing all of them to British singer Adele.

The song took several months to write, then was recorded with a different, more guitar-based arrangement that was 15 BPM faster. After hearing Mars perform the song live at the slower speed, the record label asked for a recording of the slowed-down version, which became the hit we're familiar with.

The Song

If you were going to write a straight-down-the-middle pop song, this is the way to do it. The song is unusual in that it begins right with the verse with no intro, but other than that it's formula all the way, not that there's anything wrong with that if it works (it does here). Basically the song looks like this:

verse | chorus | 2 bar interlude | verse | chorus | bridge | 2 bar interlude | verse (outro)

The good thing about "Grenade" is that it has a great melody, which is something that's sometimes sorely lacking in much of popular music. The lyrics are finely crafted and tell the age-old tale of unrequited love. They sing better than they read, but they're still put together well.

The BPM of the song is 108.

The Arrangement

Just as the form of the song follows a formula, so does the arrangement. It develops from the sparse first verse to the big chorus, then drops to a less sparse second verse, and finally peaks at the bridge. The tension is released by the stripped-down last outro verse, which is very unusual since most outros retain the big sound, and the tension, to the end.

There's an organ that plays just underneath the other instruments that acts as the Pad and glues the track together, which is a pretty common use for the instrument. What's interesting is that the arpeggiated electric piano line in the verse acts as the rhythm element, but during the chorus the rhythm switches to the double-time feel of the drums.

The song starts with a synth build and then goes right into a verse with the lead vocal in the center, arpeggiated electric piano sound on the

Photo: Brothers Le

right channel and the organ on the left. Half-way through the verse the three-part background harmonies enter along with bass drum, plus a very low in the mix tom and percussion, which propels the track forward.

In the chorus the piano is lowered in the mix and a new synth pad enters, as the drums now play a tom figure, but no snare drum. The three part background vocals behind the lead vocal act as both a fill element in the beginning of the chorus and as an additional pad element in the second half.

In the second verse, the drums continue to play the tom feel but a snare also enters. There's also a higher piano that plays effects fills, and percussion that plays fills as well. Three-part harmony is added to the lead vocal to emphasize the lyrics.

In the bridge a new higher synth pad enters, then goes to the beginning of the intro without the vocal, which resolves to the V chord and back to the chorus. The outchorus has the lead vocal adding ad-libbing to add tension. The outro is similar to the intro, only with the verse drum feel and added percussion. The song then ends on a vocal ad lib with a repeated echo effect.

Arrangement Elements
The Foundation: Bass and drums
The Pad: Organ
The Rhythm: Arpeggiated electric piano line in the verse, the double time feel of the drums in the chorus and outro, percussion
The Lead: Lead vocal
The Fills: Background vocals and the occasional percussion sound effect

The Sound

This is a very well-made record in that it's not too compressed and the ambience is layered in a pleasing, ear-candy kind of way. The vocal has a medium-long reverb decay on it in the beginning, but then a timed and repeated quarter note delay is added various times during the song. The other instruments have their own short ambiences that make them seem more in-your-face, except for the percussion effect that has a long reverb with a very long, timed pre-delay.

Listen Up

To the organ on the left and electric piano on the right of the beginning verse.

To the background vocals spread across the stereo spectrum.

To the echo on the lead vocals, which can be heard after the first chorus and bridge.

The Performance

Make no mistake about it, Bruno Mars is a star. He's got the chops and his vocal shows considerable passion that effectively sells the song. That said, this is a very well-produced song from a number of standpoints.

First of all, the song has effective dynamics, breathing in the right spaces—from the less intense verses to the big sounding choruses—then the drums play a tom pattern to add motion to the song rather than the snare, although a small sounding snare (which actually fits the song perfectly) enters in the second verse. Using the drums in this way is not only unusual, but really interesting as well.

The add to all this the use of fills to keep the listener engaged on a subliminal level. You'll find percussion, vocals, piano and synthesizers all sharing that duty. Finally, the background vocals, which are now becoming a Bruno Mars trademark, are also well-executed and add to both the motion and the tension of the song as well. This song was a huge international hit and the production is a big reason why.

The Black Eyed Peas

I Gotta Feeling

Song Facts

Album: *The E.N.D.*

Writers: The Black Eyed Peas, David Guetta, Frédéric Riesterer

Producers: David Guetta, Frédéric Riesterer

Studios: Square Productions (Paris), Metropolis (London)

Release Date: May 21, 2009

Length: 4:50 (album), 4:05 (single edit)

Sales: 11+ million

Highest Chart Position: #1 U.S. *Billboard* Hot 100, #1 U.K. Singles Chart, #1 in Australia, Austria, Belgium, Brazil, Canada, Denmark, Greece, Ireland, Italy, Israel, Mexico, Netherlands, New Zealand, Romania, Sweden, and Switzerland

"I Gotta Feeling" is the second single from *The E.N.D.*, the fifth studio album from The Black Eyed Peas. The song spent 14 weeks at the top of the *Billboard* Hot 100 and went on to sell eight million digital singles, a record still held in the United States. The song was nominated for a Grammy award for Record of the Year, and it won for Best Pop Performance by a Duo or Group with Vocals.

The song was admittedly based around the chords of U2's "I'll Go Crazy If I Don't Go Crazy Tonight" and was produced by French superstar DJ/producer/artist David Guetta.

Photo: Eddie Malluk/atlasicons.com

The Song

"I Gotta Feeling" has an unusual form in that the sections don't always come where you expect them and sometimes have different lengths.

The form looks like this:

intro | chorus (32 bars) | verse (24 bars) | B section | chorus (16 bars) | verse (16 bars) | B section | verse (16 bars) | chorus | end

What's interesting is that the longest verse and chorus actually occur at the beginning of the song, and the second B section is in between the second and third verses.

The melody is both singable and infectious, but the lyrics leave something to be desired. It's a party song and the words reflect that well, but they're not particularly well crafted, although that's not necessarily what you're looking for from a song by The Black Eyed Peas.

The BPM of the song is 128.

The Arrangement

Just as with the form, the arrangement of "I Gotta Feeling" is also somewhat different than what you'd expect from a pop hit. While it does breathe dynamically like most hits, it doesn't happen when you expect it to.

At about 30 seconds in length, the intro is exceptionally long for a hit. It begins with a quarter-note synth over a low bass-string pad for 8 bars, and then on the second 8 bars, a high string part enters. At that point, the chorus begins. The vocal melody line enters along with a clean electric guitar playing sixteenth notes, and the low and high string parts exit. The third time through the pattern, Fergie's vocal enters an octave higher than the lead, along with a sixteenth-note bass synth, claps on beats 2 and 4, and a hi-hat playing a sixteenth-note pattern. On the fourth and last time through the pattern, the guitar part is doubled.

A snare drum pickup takes us into the verse, where the kick enters playing the familiar "4 on the floor" beat, a steady quarter-note pulse common to dance music, with claps on beats 2 and 4 and a hi-hat playing a sixteenth-note figure. Two additional synths enter as well, one playing a high figure and another playing the upbeats. On bar 9, Fergie comes in with a sung melody, and then at bar 17, the other Peas enter for a rap. The music also stops on beat 4 of bar 19 and beat 3 of bar 21 to add tension and development; this leads into the B section, where the instrumentation is identical to the verse except for the vocals.

On the second chorus, the arrangement reverts to the intro with a high synth playing eighth notes over a low synth pad. The second time through the pattern on bar 9, the high string line enters along with Fergie's octave vocal and the "woo-hoo" answers.

On the next verse, the instrumentation continues from the chorus but with a new quarter-note "white-noise" part that acts almost like the snare, a new sixteenth-note synth line, and answers to the vocal phrases. On bar 9, another synth pad and high string line add tension going into the B section, which is the same as the verse except for the vocals. There is a build on the last 4 bars, though, culminating with a synth whoosh and snare drum fill that lead into another verse, where the drums reenter. At bar 9, a new mid-range synth enters on the upbeats.

As with many dance songs, the music of the verse continues with the chorus sung over it, and on the last 8 bars, the claps are emphasized a bit more. The song ends on a panning synthesizer and a dry-sounding vocal.

Arrangement Elements
The Foundation: Kick, low synth
The Rhythm: Hi-hat, eighth- and sixteenth-note synths, upbeat synth
The Pad: Low synth on intro and second chorus
The Lead: Lead vocals and raps
The Fills: Vocal answers

The Sound

Just like the song form and arrangement, the sound of "I Gotta Feeling" is different too. First of all, it vacillates between wet and dry on the vocals. The sung vocals have a long-delayed reverb, which is mixed low in the first chorus but is more noticeable during the second, and the rapped vocals go between processed and unprocessed throughout the song. The synths also have some ambience on them, but it's timed to the track and mixed low so it's never obvious.

While most of "I Gotta Feeling" is panned to the center, the vocals—especially when the entire group is singing—are panned slightly to either side; while single answer fills are sometimes radically panned, keeping the listener's attention without their knowing why. Likewise, some of the higher-register synths are in stereo and panned slightly left or right, except for the very last one at the end of the song, which sounds like it has an auto-pan as it travels from right to left and back again.

"I Gotta Feeling" is very compressed but it doesn't feel like it, and that's the sign of a great mixing job. All of the elements sit in the mix where you can hear them, with nothing being masked by anything else.

Listen Up

To the reverb added to Fergie's voice at 1:55.

To the vocals that bounce back and forth between the speakers at 1:58.

To the reverb tail on the end of the vocals.

To the arpeggiated synth on the third verse at 3:00.

T… …DUCTION

…eeling" seems to break all the rules of making a hit, from the …time before the vocal enters (30 seconds) to when the main beat of the song begins (1:30) to the odd form and arrangement. That being said, it has what is common to all hits: it's interesting and has dynamics. There's always some new part jumping in before you can get bored, whether it be a new synth or vocal. Plus, changing the vocals from wet to dry to wet again is a very powerful tool for keeping the listener's attention.

Likewise, the song's dynamics shift constantly, from less intense to more intense to less to most—another sign of great production. As an aside, this is another example of a song without a traditional bass guitar, instead centering the low end of the frequency range around the low synthesizer and kick drum.

50 Cent
In da Club

Song Facts

Album: *Get Rich or Die Tryin'*
Writers: Curtis Jackson, Andre Young, Mike Elizondo
Producers: Dr. Dre, Mike Elizondo
Studio: Record One Studios (Sherman Oaks, CA)
Release Date: January 7, 2003
Length: 3:12
Sales: 500,000+ (single), 12+ million worldwide (album)
Highest Chart Position: #1 U.S. *Billboard* Hot 100, #3 U.K. Singles Chart, #3 in Australia, Austria, Belgium, Denmark, Finland, Germany, Greece, Ireland, Netherlands, Norway, Sweden, and Switzerland

"In da Club" is the first single from 50 Cent's debut album, *Get Rich or Die Tryin'*. The song was a big hit, remaining at #1 on *Billboard*'s Hot 100 chart for nine weeks. It was eventually nominated for Grammy awards in the categories of Best Male Rap Solo Performance and Best Rap Song. "In da Club" was also listed as #24 on *Billboard*'s Hot 100 Songs of the Decade and #448 on *Rolling Stone*'s list of 500 Greatest Songs of All Time.

The track was written and created by producers Dr. Dre (Andre Young) and Mike Elizondo, and was originally intended for the hip-hop group D12, who passed. "In da Club" was one of seven songs that 50 Cent recorded in a marathon five-day session with Dre.

Photo: Anthony Cutajar/atlasicons.com

The Song

"In da Club" is one of the few hip-hop songs with a defined bridge, even though it's over the same beat as the rest of the song. The song form looks like this:

intro | verse | chorus | verse | chorus | bridge | verse | chorus | outro

The lyrics in the hook and chorus are strong, even though not all of the listening audience can really relate to the lyrics in the rest of the song.

The BPM of this song is 90.

The Arrangement

The intro to "In da Club" is 2 bars of the verse, which is followed by a short 6-bar verse. The chorus is the same each of the three times it's featured in the song, with the lyrics repeated twice each time. The chorus is different from the verse in that the keyboard "string" line is moved up an octave for the entire section, and the rap is doubled. The octave section also appears at bar 9 for 2 bars of each verse.

The 4-bar bridge changes, as there's a descending string line that acts as a pad, then the final verse is only 12 bars long, making up the 16 bars between choruses. The outro is the music track minus the rap, which repeats for a long fade of more than a minute.

The only other deviation in the basic music track is a guitar that enters halfway through the second verse and exits after the bridge. The guitar reenters at the final chorus and remains for the rest of the song.

Arrangement Elements
The Foundation: Bass and drums
The Rhythm: Hi-hat, guitar, main string line
The Pad: None
The Lead: Rap
The Fills: Rap answers

The Sound

The sound of "In da Club" is pretty basic; there aren't many instruments or vocals, and there's very little sonic manipulation. Everything in the mix is totally free from effects, with the exception of the string lines, which appear to have some ambience that's part of the original string sample. This is an excellent example of how less is more.

What is unusual for a rap song is that the vocals are doubled in each chorus and then spread slightly left and right in the stereo soundfield. In fact, just about everything is in mono, even the programmed drums. The bass is also very low and subtle, almost like part of the kick drum sound except that the pitch changes with every beat.

Listen Up

To how the vocals are doubled and spread left and right in the choruses.

To how most of the music is in mono.

The Production

Much of the brilliance of producer Dr. Dre is in knowing when to stop a production and a mix. Take the music bed, for example. The programmed drums are just a very simple beat repeated over and over throughout the song. There are no variations or fills. The song is basic and very solid, with only a clap added to the snare to make it sound different.

The same can be said for the main repeating string riff, in which the only variation is that the line is played an octave higher during part of the verses and choruses. Much like the drums, the bass is a repeating line that never varies through the song.

When it was time to mix, once again there was nothing fancy—the mix was balanced and that was it. Dre knew that the song would sell itself. "In da Club" would no doubt be more sophisticated in the hands of another producer, but that doesn't mean it would be any better.

Ellie Goulding

Lights

Song Facts

Album: *Lights*

Writers: Ellie Goulding, Richard Stannard, Ash Howes

Producer: Richard "Biff" Stannard

Release Date: March 13, 2011

Length: 4:05

Sales: 4+ million

Highest Chart Position: #1 U.S. *Billboard* Pop Songs, #2 Billboard Hot 100, #1 Polish Airplay Chart

Ellie Goulding's "Lights," the title song from the album of the same name (*Lights*), was the sixth hit single from the album in the U.K., but a sleeper hit in America. Although the single was certified platinum in the U.S. in May of 2012 with sales of 1.9 million, it spent 33 weeks on the chart before reaching its high point at #2 on the Hot 100.

"Lights" is also another example of a song that was never expected to be a hit. Originally just a bonus track on the iTunes edition of her debut album, the song was re-edited for inclusion on her *Bright Lights* album, a repackaged *Lights* with six new tracks. In fact, Goulding was already working on her next album when the song took a surprise turn up the charts, thanks to the millions of views on YouTube.

The album *Lights* hit #1 on the British charts but topped out at #21 on the U.S. *Billboard* 200 and #12 on the Digital Albums chart. It has sold more than 1.6 million copies worldwide.

The Song

"Lights" has a slightly unusual form in the there's both a verse B section and a chorus B section. The form looks like this:

intro | verse | B section | chorus | chorus B section | verse | B section | chorus | chorus B section | bridge | chorus (no vocals) | chorus | chorus B section | outro | intro

What happens is that the chorus hook comes back in after the chorus B section, which makes the chorus a lot longer than normal.

The bridge is also interesting in that it's instrumental, followed by an instrumental first half of the next chorus. This is a way to add both length and interest to the song.

The song has a pretty strong melody in every section, and, what is unusual for a pop song these days, it differs considerably from section to section. The lyrics paint an abstract picture about Goulding's real-life fear of the dark, but the rhymes don't seem forced, even though the content may be a little thin.

The BPM of the song is 120.

The Arrangement

Like most hits, the arrangement for "Lights" is based around each section changing both instrument-wise and dynamically.

The song begins with an arpeggiated synth by itself, then is joined on the verse by the lead vocal. There are no additional instruments until the chorus, when both a synth bass and a high pad enter along with doubled male and lead vocals. The kick drum enters on the chorus B section.

On the second verse the song breaks down again to the arpeggiated synth, but programmed drums and a strumming guitar are added as well. The second B section also includes a high harmony of the melody line. The second chorus has the drums continue playing (unlike the first chorus) and an additional synth pad is added.

The bridge is another breakdown back to the drums and arpeggiated synth, but a cello-like synth plays the melody, which all ends in a vinyl record-like slowdown. The chorus then begins with the same instrumentation as the second chorus, with the addition of a tom fill and the vocals singing only "Lights," which ends in another slowdown.

The third chorus then continues with the same instrumentation including the tom fills. The outro is over the chorus chord pattern with the same instruments, but the background vocals again sing "Lights." The lead vocal ad libs, and on the third time through the pattern the chord changes go up instead of down. The song ends just as it began, with the lone arpeggiated synth.

Arrangement Elements
The Foundation: Programmed drums, synth bass
The Rhythm: Arpeggiated synth and rhythm guitar on verses
The Pad: Low and very high synths in the choruses and bridge
The Lead: Vocal
The Fills: Vocal answers

The Sound

Unlike so many pop songs these days, the sound of "Lights" is pretty clean with little distortion. There are no overt ambiences, except for the many delays that occur on the vocals and the ping-pong delay on the arpeggiated synth. The vocal is very breathy and in-your-face, and you can hear the sibilance because of the compression, but it certainly works with the track. The toms aren't as forward as they are in some mixes and they sound somewhat mellower than they might normally sound in other songs of this type, but this works well to push the motion of the song along without it being in the way and competing with the vocal. All in all, it's a really good sounding recording.

Listen Up

To the delays on the lead vocal that occur on only one side of the soundfield.

To the doubled lead vocals in the chorus that are spread left and right.

To the stutter edits on the vocal on the outro.

The Production

Like most hits, it's the many little things that sometime make a production, like the doubled lead vocals with the low male vocals in the chorus to develop the sound and make it bigger. Listen to how the song builds in the chorus, then breathes a bit with fewer instruments during the verse, which is an example of great song dynamics. Listen to how the song's second verse builds with a vocal answer, then the entrance of strings, then harmony vocals. Hear how the toms in the last chorus add motion to the song the same way the rhythm guitar does in the verse. These are the things that keep a song interesting, an element that's vital in all hits.

Lady Gaga

Poker Face

Song Facts

Album: *The Fame*

Writers: Stefani Germanotta, Nadir Khayat

Producer: RedOne

Studio: Record Plant Recording Studios (Los Angeles)

Release Date: September 23, 2008

Length: 3:58

Sales: 10+ million (single), 15+ million (album)

Highest Chart Position: #1 U.S. *Billboard* Hot 100, #1 U.K. Singles Chart, #1 in Australia, Belgium, Canada, Finland, France, Germany, Mexico, Norway, Sweden, and Switzerland

"Poker Face," from Lady Gaga's debut album *The Fame*, was the song that catapulted her to international stardom. The song was #1 virtually worldwide and became one of the biggest-selling singles of all time at over 10 million. It was nominated for both Record of the Year and Song of the Year at the 2010 Grammy awards, and won for Best Dance Recording. *Rolling Stone* ranked it #93 of the 100 Best Songs of the 2000s, while *NME* placed it at #103 of the 150 Best Tracks of the Past 15 Years.

The album was a huge hit as well, peaking at #2 but staying in the U.S. *Billboard* Hot 200 for an unbelievable 100 non-consecutive weeks. It was nominated for six Grammy awards and won for Best Electronic/ Dance Album. It also won Best International Album at the 2010 BRIT Awards.

The Song

"Poker Face" was a huge hit for Lady Gaga, and a close listen to the song tells you exactly why: it has everything we've come to expect from a mega-hit. First of all, the song form may be pretty basic, but it's expertly put together to keep the interest high, since there's always forward motion and dynamics. The form looks like this:

intro | verse | B section | chorus | interlude | verse | B section | chorus | interlude
bridge | chorus | chorus | chorus | interlude/chorus | interlude/chorus | interlude/chorus

What's especially interesting is that both the bridge and interlude/choruses at the end of the song are primarily choruses with either new parts or a combination of new and previously heard parts. It's a great way to keep things familiar yet different.

The melody is strong and memorable, and the lyrics are far superior to most pop songs in that they tell a story and are cleverly put together.

The BPM of this song is 119.

The Arrangement

"Poker Face" begins with a single arpeggiated synth that makes up the backbone of the song, and it's followed by an additional synth layer playing the same part. Then, the song's hook enters along with a new synth line. After the line plays through once (4 bars), it plays through a second time—with kick, claps, and open hi-hat—to end the intro.

When the lead vocal enters at the verse, only the kick and basic arpeggiating synth remain for the first half. At bar 9, the synth line from the intro enters, as does a very subtle percussion sound.

A new synth enters on beat 1 of the B section to signify the beginning of the section, but other than the vocal changing, the instruments remain the same until the downbeat of the last bar, when the music stops except for a combination of a guitar-string-scratch glissando and a synth whoosh sound.

On the chorus, all the instruments reenter with the addition of a string pad, claps, open hi-hat, and a new synth emphasizing the upbeats. The vocal sings the chorus hook and the background vocals answer. At the interlude, the strings, claps, and hi-hat all drop out, and a new synth plays only on the downbeat of the first measure.

Unusually, the second verse, B section, chorus, and interlude are all the same as the first with no changes. The bridge begins again with the same instrumentation as the interlude, only with a new synth line that plays by itself for 4 bars and is then joined by Gaga's sing/talk for another 8 bars.

The last chorus then begins, but without the drums for 4 bars while you hear the guitar-string-scratch glissando. The drums enter while Gaga sings, and later a lower harmony is added. The song then goes into the interlude lyric over the chorus instruments and chord changes, and the song ends on the last phrase of the answer.

Arrangement Elements
The Foundation: Kick drum
The Rhythm: Synthesizer, claps
The Pad: Strings during the chorus
The Lead: Lead vocal
The Fills: Background vocals

The Sound

What strikes you most about the sonics of "Poker Face" is the use of echo to set the ambience. The prominent long delay that's timed to the track (probably a quarter-note delay) fills up the space where there's no vocal and at the ends of phrases on both the lead and background vocals. One place where it can be clearly heard is the male vocal exclamation after the end of the first phrase of the second verse, where you can distinctly hear the echo ping back and forth between the speakers. This can also be heard on the lead vocal on the second B section.

It's also interesting that Gaga's verse vocals are doubled but not very closely, which produces an interesting effect. This especially sets up the bridge, when the vocal is only a single track, making it sound much different from the vocal on the rest of the song.

The panorama of the soundfield is also put to great use in "Poker Face" by having some elements strictly in mono and others in stereo. For instance, the synth line in the intro and bridge is in stereo, and that provides a lot of space for the lead vocal as a result. The background vocal answers are all in stereo, while the drum elements of kick, snare, and cymbals are all in the center.

Finally, the mix balance is interesting because there's no real bass instrument, so the kick drum uses up much of that sonic space. The fact that there are a number of synthesizers parts more or less from the same family of sound (possibly even the same instrument) yet all are easily distinguishable is a tribute to a great mix by engineer Robert Orton.

Listen Up

To the synth that plays only on the upbeats of the chorus.

To the cross echoes on the lead vocal during the second verse.

To the guitar-string-scratch glissandos and synth sound effects at the turnarounds between verse and chorus.

The Production

"Poker Face" is evidence of the new sound of pop-hit production, which no longer depends on a bass guitar to fill out the bottom end of the frequency range. The song was produced by RedOne and is entirely programmed except for the vocals. Where once upon a time that meant the song would be stiff and robot-like, "Poker Face" is imminently danceable with a terrific feel, and it breathes as parts enter and are removed.

As with all hits, the details are what make the song. Take, for instance, the harmony answer vocals in the chorus, which are pretty subtle but really lift the song and almost sound like a harmony vocal to the lead. The low harmony part on the pre-chorus (the B section) also helps to develop the dynamics of the song. Add these subtleties to the gigantic groove and you have a massive hit.

LMFAO

Sexy and I Know It

Song Facts

Album: *Sorry for Party Rocking*

Writers: Stefan "Redfoo" Gordy, David Listenbee, Erin Beck, George Robertson, Kenny "Audiobot" Oliver

Producer: Party Rock

Release Date: September 21, 2011

Length: 3:19

Sales: 7+ million

Highest Chart Position: #1 *Billboard* Hot 100, #1 in four other countries

LMFAO's "Sexy and I Know It" was a worldwide Top 10 hit in more than 15 countries and was the third single from the group's *Sorry for Party Rocking* album. While it may go unnoticed by many who don't like the dance or Top 40 genre, LMFAO's sound is pretty groundbreaking. Why? They're a great example of the marriage of electronic music (their sub-genre is known as "hip house") to a catchy melody and lyrics, which has caused the group to break through in a big way.

The LMFAO duo consists of Redfoo and Skyblu, both descendants of Motown Records founder Berry Gordy Jr. It was Redfoo's best friend, will.i.am from the Black Eyed Peas, who introduced them to Interscope Records head Jimmy Iovine; they were immediately signed to a record deal. The demos that they turned in were so close to finished products that little additional work was required.

"Sexy and I Know It" was used in several commercials, the biggest one being an M&M's commercial for Superbowl 2012. The song was even

California
I WRKOUT

used in a *Sesame Street* parody called "I'm Elmo and I Know It," and as the theme song for a Chilean telenovela called Las Vega's.

The Song

Looking at "Sexy and I Know It" from a pop perspective, the song is simplistic both in form and in its lyrics, but as this is a completely new genre we can throw conventional thinking out the window. All dance and electronic music are built around 4- and 8-bar modules which sometimes work as a traditional verse, chorus, bridge formula, but then again, sometimes they don't. In this song they do, and that's why it's such a big pop hit. Here's what the form looks like:

intro | verse | B section | chorus | verse | B section |
chorus | verse | B section | chorus

Pretty simple, right? Not exactly. The verse after the second chorus is a hybrid; it's a little bit of a verse with the song hook thrown in. You could almost call it a bridge, but only from a lyric standpoint since the underlying musical structure doesn't change.

The lyrics are never going to win any awards, but at least the song has lyrics, which many songs in this genre lack. Of course, the hook is extremely strong, which is the key to any hit.

The BPM of the song is 132.

The Arrangement

This song shows that you can have a hit with a minimum number of elements. As with all electronic music, the rhythm is the most important element, but seldom is it so stripped down as this throughout the entire song. The song consists of kick drum, the vocal, a repeating synth line, and very few synth and drum fill elements; it's really disassembled almost as far as it can be, yet it still works.

The song begins with kick drum, an arpeggiated synth line, a clap-like noise in stereo, and a white noise that goes from bright to mellow. On the verse, everything drops out except for the arpeggiated synth, and the vocal enters. On the B section a distorted hi-hat enters as well as a new doubled vocal and "Aah's" on the downbeat of each bar.

The chorus is different from what you usually hear in that the synth becomes more mellow sounding, the arpeggiated line changes, and a snare gradually builds to a roll. The kick then reenters along with the original arpeggiated synth, and handclaps are added on bar 5.

On the second verse the synth line and the kick continue along with stereo claps, and ad lib vocals in the holes between phrases from bar 5 onward. The B section continues just like the previous one except for the addition of the kick. The second chorus is identical to the first except that the synth sound and register changes to something brighter and higher.

The next verse continues on with the same sounds as the chorus except that the lyrics are changed. The outro changes back to the original B section with the addition of a new synth note on the "2 and" and "4 and," which gradually has more reverb added to it as it gets closer to the end of the song. The ending is on the vocal hook with a reverbed out synth note and delayed hat with fading repeats.

Arrangement Elements
The Foundation: Kick drum sample
The Rhythm: Kick drum, high hat, repeating synth line
The Pad: None
The Lead: Vocal
The Fills: Various synth sounds and noises

THE SOUND

With electronic music, sound quality is never an issue since noise and distortion can be welcome elements. The most important sound element is the beat, which is driven by the bass drum sound. Since there are so few musical elements, the kick has to be very large to fill the frequency space and this one certainly is. The vocals all have a distorted edge to them, which, as previously mentioned, is okay in this type of music and even desired. Everything is dry and in-your-face except for the repeating synth, which is delayed at the end of the song along with the hi-hat sound. Of course, it's all compressed as much as possible.

Listen Up

To the vocals in the verse which are doubled and panned slightly left and right, but then sometimes go to the center for just a phrase.

To the stereo noise on the intro that goes from mellow to bright.

To the short stereo slap delay on the lead vocal. The left side is mellow and the right is bright.

To the synth hit on the "2 and" and "4 and" on the outro.

THE PRODUCTION

Any song that can be interesting with so few elements has to have pretty good production. In this case, the song has a great beat for dancing and a hook that will stick in your mind, which is the reason it's a hit. The two most consistent elements, the bass drum and repeating synth sounds, keep changing with every section and sometimes within the same section. The very subtle entrance of additional elements keep your attention. That's the essence of good production in a nutshell.

Justin Timberlake

SexyBack

Song Facts

Album: *FutureSex/LoveSounds*

Writers: Justin Timberlake, Timothy Mosley, Nate Hills

Producers: Justin Timberlake, Timbaland, Danja

Studio: Thomas Crown Studio (Virginia Beach, VA)

Release Date: July 7, 2006

Length: 4:03

Sales: 4 million (single), 10+ million (album)

Highest Chart Position: #1 U.S. *Billboard* Hot 100, #1 U.K. Singles Chart, #1 European Hot 100 Singles, #1 in Australia, Germany, Ireland, New Zealand, and Norway

"SexyBack" was one of the first songs recorded for Justin Timberlake's second solo album, *FutureSex/LoveSounds*. The song was an experiment for Timberlake, who wanted it to sound like Bowie or Prince doing a cover version of James Brown's 1970 hit "Sex Machine." It's also one of the few Timberlake songs that doesn't feature his trademark falsetto voice.

The song became Timberlake's first #1 on *Billboard*'s Hot 100 chart, where it spent seven consecutive weeks, and eventually claimed a 2007 Grammy award for Best Dance Recording. The album was equally successful, being nominated for two Grammys and hitting the Top 5 in most countries.

Photo: George Chin/atlasicons.com

The Song

In "SexyBack," basically the same sections are repeated over and over. Originally titled "Be Gone With It," the song was deemed to be without a hook (which it still doesn't really have). It was Timberlake's idea to rename the song "SexyBack." The title is stated right at the beginning of the song, and this takes your mind immediately away from the idea of a traditional hook in the chorus.

It many ways, the song seems to have three separate choruses, but the form looks like this:

intro | verse | B section (bridge) | chorus | verse | B section (bridge) | chorus | verse | B section (bridge) | chorus | interlude | verse | chorus | outro (fade)

What is referred to as the "bridge" in the lyrics is really more of a B section, as it's labeled above, since it precedes a chorus and isn't a peak of the song.

"SexyBack" is a pure dance song, and even though it has a melody, there's not much harmonic movement; basically, there's just one chordal riff over which the melody repeats throughout the song. Likewise, there's not much going on with the lyrics, which are repeated over and over with only very slight changes.

The BPM of the song is 118.

The Arrangement

The song begins with an 8-bar intro (which is just a verse without the vocals) before the lead vocal and answer vocals enter on the verse. The B section introduces congas for some added motion, as the vocal melody changes from more of a spoken part to one sung in Timberlake's higher range.

In the chorus, the synth changes to a single-bar pattern, which is doubled by the bass (although it's low in the mix). At bar 9 (halfway through the chorus), a guitar appears on the left side along with three-part harmony background vocals in stereo.

The second verse, B section, and chorus are identical to the first except for a slight lyric change in the verse; but at the end of the second chorus, the song breaks down to just drums, percussion, guitar, and a sampled vocal.

The song then proceeds to another verse, which is identical to the previous ones except for another slight lyric change. This time, instead of going to a B section, the song goes to the chorus instead, which, again, is the same as the previous ones.

The outro is a bit different. It's 4 bars of chorus backing track, with the vocal from the bridge. The song then slows to a stop (thanks to the Avid Pro Tools Vari-Fi plug-in) and proceeds into a long fade with the guitar from the chorus and a slightly different synth line.

Arrangement Elements
The Foundation: Drum machine kick and finger snaps, synth, bass in chorus
The Rhythm: Drum machine percussion, guitar
The Pad: None
The Lead: Lead vocal
The Fills: Answer vocals, background harmonies

The Sound

The sonic element that stands out more than any other on "SexyBack" is the distorted vocals, which came by way of the iZotope Trash plug-in and an old MXR flanger, according to engineer Jimmy Douglass. Although everything sounds relatively dry and in-your-face, if you listen closely, you can hear a very short delay with a bit of room reverb on the lead and answer vocals, with the background harmonies just a getting a little more.

There's a moderate amount of compression on each of the instruments, but the song never sounds overly squashed—although much of that could be due to the distortion on the vocals. The stereo field isn't very wide, with the drums in the center and the synth in stereo along with the background and doubled answer vocals.

Listen Up

To the guitar on the left side during the chorus.

To the doubled background vocal answers in the verse and B sections.

To the stereo background vocal harmonies on the second half of the choruses.

To the short "Elvis-style" delay on the lead vocal, heard clearly during the first verse.

The Production

"SexyBack" is a song that was created, tracked, and mixed in one day, so it's a tribute to spontaneity and knowing when to say "Stop, we're good" (a rare trait in producers these days). There aren't a lot of instrumental parts, and what's there either adds to the beat or the motion. Perhaps the only exception to that is the 12 tracks of three-part harmony background vocals (according to engineer Jimmy Douglass) that you hear in the choruses; but even that never feels over-produced, like so many other records. Of course, the choice of a distorted vocal sound is a bold one that only someone as successful as Justin Timberlake could make without a record label asking for a cleaner version, but that's also part of the winning vision of the producers.

Nicki Minaj

Super Bass

Song Facts

Album: *Pink Friday*

Writers: Onika Maraj, Daniel Johnson, Ester Dean, Roahn Hylton

Producers: Kane Beatz, JMIKE

Studios: 54 Sound Studios (Detroit), Chalice Recording Studios (Los Angeles), Glenwood Place Studios (Burbank, CA)

Release Date: April 5, 2011

Length: 3:19

Sales: 5+ million

Highest Chart Position: #2 U.S. *Billboard* Rap Songs, #3 U.S. Pop Songs, #3 U.S. *Billboard* Hot 100

Nicki Minaj's "Super Bass" was the fifth single from her debut album *Pink Friday*. The song draws from R&B, hip-hop, and electronic music, fusing all those genres into the perfect pop tune. "Super Bass" reached #3 on the *Billboard* Hot 100 chart, and was an even bigger online hit, with the video getting over 250 million views. It has sold more than four million copies to date, becoming one of the biggest recent sellers.

The album *Pink Friday* sold over a million copies and hit #1 on the *Billboard* 200 chart. It also garnered Minaj three 2012 Grammy nominations for Best New Artist, Best Rap Performance and Best Rap Album.

"Super Bass" went Top 10 in ten countries, and the song's success in the U.K. led *Pink Friday* to be renamed *Super Bass Edition* when the deluxe version of the album was released.

The Song

"Super Bass" is a pretty straightforward pop song with the standard three sections: verse, chorus, and bridge. The form looks like this:

intro | verse | chorus | verse | chorus | bridge | chorus

No section is repeated and the song has a hard ending, which has now become the norm for a pop song. The most unusual aspect of the song form is that there's a breakdown halfway during the chorus for 4 bars, then the hook is repeated for the last 4.

There won't be any awards won for the lyrics of this song (like many others in this genre), but pop songs are usually sold on their hooks, not their lyrics, and "Super Bass" has a good one.

The BPM of the song is 125.

The Arrangement

The arrangement of "Super Bass" is different than most pop songs. The song begins with a short intro where a chorused electric guitar with an autofilter (sort of an automatic wah that opens and closes with the dynamics of the playing) plays a line (which is never heard again in the song, by the way) over a low piano pad, a high arpeggiated string part, and percussion. Halfway through, Minaj enters with the vocals. The song then breaks down to an electric piano pad, tuned percussion, and synth bass. Throughout the song, claps are used instead of a snare drum for the song's pulse.

For the chorus, the bass enters playing quarter notes, and the eighth-note arpeggiated string line plays again. The claps are doubled while the kick plays a four-on-the-floor pattern for the first 4 bars, then plays a "boom daboom" pattern for the rest of the section. The second verse is identical to the first except for the arpeggiated strings that enter halfway through the verse. The second chorus is identical to the first.

The bridge starts with a breakdown that features a 16th-note synth over a lower pad. The claps enter on the third bar, and the kick and quarter-note arpeggiated strings enter at bar 5 and remain in the song for the rest of the section. The last chorus is identical to the first.

What's interesting is that "Super Bass" is one of the few songs where the choruses remain identical throughout the song. Usually additional instruments enter over the course of the song, making the last chorus much bigger sounding than the first, but that's not the case here.

Arrangement Elements
The Foundation: Bass synth, kick, high hat, claps
The Rhythm: Tuned percussion, arpeggiated synths
The Pad: Synth pads, synth bass, electric piano
The Lead: Lead vocals, guitar in the intro
The Fills: Background vocals in the second verse

The Sound

"Super Bass" has a very modern, layered mix, meaning that the mix elements are put into different sonic environments with the help of effects such as reverb and delay. The stereo electric piano (which plays throughout the song) is pretty dry as is the hi-hat, but most other mix elements have some sort of effect, which pushes them further back in the mix depth-wise. The arpeggiated strings seem to have a timed delay on them which is different from the vocal.

The song is very compressed, although most of it does sound pretty natural as you don't hear any pumping or breathing or compressor artifacts, especially in the vocal. Although most mixers and mastering engineers compress a pop song as standard operating procedure these days to make it as loud as possible, "Super Bass" would probably sound a lot better with a little more natural dynamics—although there probably isn't much to begin with considering that all the musical elements except the vocals, intro guitar sound, and maybe the electric piano sound like they're programmed.

The vocal has both a long reverb and a fairly long timed delay that you can't hear during the verses and chorus, but are very apparent during the bridge.

Listen Up

To the vocals in the chorus as they're doubled and spread slightly to the left and right.

To the arpeggiated strings that enter halfway through the second verse.

To the tuned percussion and how it pushes the song along.

To the electric piano and how it glues everything together.

To the cymbal swells at the beginning of the song and end of the bridge.

The Production

This song is made for Top 40 radio. It's catchy, with a pretty good hook, but oddly, it never settles into a groove. At the beginning of every chorus when the kick begins with a four on the floor, it begins to groove, only to deviate from it after 4 bars. This is quite unusual for any Top 40 hit, especially one aimed at the dance community, yet here it is, still a hit.

That said, there's a lot more going on than meets the ear. The tuned percussion, the electric piano pad, the arpeggiated strings in the chorus, and the cymbal swells all work together to make a rather simple tune become a hit.

David Guetta

Turn Me On

Song Facts

Album: *Nothing But the Beat*

Writers: Ester Dean, Onika Maraj, David Guetta, Giorgio Tuinfort

Producers: David Guetta, Giorgio Tuinfort, Black Raw

Studios: Gum Prod Studios, Catfield Studios (Paris), Piano Music Studio (Amsterdam), Can Rocas Studio (Ibiza, Spain)

Release Date: January 27, 2012

Length: 3:19

Sales: 3+ million

Highest Chart Position: #1 *Billboard* Hot Dance Club Songs, #1 Poland

Here's a song that's at the tip of a trend in music that's starting to snowball. The song is "Turn Me On" by French DJ David Guetta, featuring singer Nicki Minaj. Electronic dance music has been a huge underground scene for several years and we've seen flashes of it on the Top 40 charts, but now it's beginning to break through in a big way and David Guetta is leading the charge by incorporating star vocalists into what was once purely electronic music.

Guetta was one of the trailblazers of this trend, particularly on his 2009 album *One Love*, which included hit singles "When Love Takes Over" (featuring Kelly Rowland), "Gettin' over You" (featuring Chris Willis, Fergie, and LMFAO) and "Sexy Bitch" (featuring Akon). The last song hit the Top 5 in the United States and all three singles reached #1 in the U.K. The album also featured another international hit single "Memories" (featuring Kid Cudi), which was a Top 5 hit in many countries. Guetta

Photo: Larry Marano/atlasicons.com

has sold over 3 million albums and 15 million singles worldwide and is one of the most sought-after producers in the music business.

The Song

"Turn Me On" has a very basic song form with one twist in the prechorus. The form looks like this:

intro | verse | B section | interlude | chorus | verse | B section | interlude | chorus | bridge | chorus

Every section is 8 bars long except for the interlude (the "Oh" part before the chorus) which is only 4 bars, and that's the only thing that changes the song up form-wise.

Once again, the lyrics won't win any awards, but do you really expect them to in a pop song like this?

The BPM of the song is 125.

The Arrangement

In keeping with the nature of electronic dance music, there aren't a lot of elements or layers to the song. Instead of a drum kit and bass, the rhythm element is made up of a huge kick drum and a bass sound, which take up so much sonic space that's it would be difficult to fit additional foundation instruments in.

What's very interesting in "Turn Me On" is the way the claps and hihat are used to develop the song. Usually a hit is developed by adding additional arrangement elements or additional instrument or vocal layers. On this song, percussion is used to accomplish the same thing. Here's how it's done: In the first verse you only hear the kick and bass sounds, but doubled claps in stereo are used to develop the B section.

In verse 2 the claps continue, but a hi-hat sound is used to develop the second B section.

The song begins with a stereo synth line which then leads right into the verse that has a kick drum and synth bass. At the B section, stereo claps are introduced and the vocals are doubled. On the interlude the song breaks down to just a single vocal that pans from left to right and back again as it modulates into distortion while a low synth pad gurgles underneath and the kick drum builds.

On the first half of the chorus, synth chords enter along with a small natural sounding drum kit, along with harmony vocals. On the second half the big sounding kick and synth bass are reintroduced along with a high-hat.

The next verse is the same as the first except for the introduction of stereo claps, a bigger synth playing between the vocal phrases, and the vocal changing the melody slightly before the B section. The second B section is slightly different from the first, with bigger claps and a hi-hat. The next interlude is identical to the first as is the next chorus.

The bridge breaks down into a new synth pad, which then leads into a rap where only the kick plays along with an organ sound and a soft bass synth. The last chorus is identical to the previous choruses instrument-wise, except for the fact that it's half as long. The song ends on sound effects.

Arrangement Elements
The Foundation: Bass and kick sounds
The Rhythm: Arpeggiated synth line, claps from the first B section onward, high hat sound in the second B section
The Pad: Synth in the bridge
The Lead: Vocal
The Fills: Background vocal line at the end of the chorus, arpeggiated synth in the choruses, vocal answers in the first half of the bridge

The Sound

Another function of electronic dance music is the fact that distortion is normally viewed as something to be embraced and not rejected. There's plenty of it here, and even the vocal (which you'd expect to be clean) has a lot of distortion.

There's a slight ambience sound on most of the synths, but most of the layering on both the synths and vocals comes from timed delays that are long enough to hear. This fills in the holes between phrases.

Listen Up

To the way the vocal is manipulated in the interludes by panning from left to right channel and back again, all the while modulating gradually into full distortion at the end.

To the stereo claps that enter in the first B section.

To the small-sounding drum kit sound at the beginning of the choruses.

To the quarter-note delay on lead vocal.

The Production

A big reason why this song was a hit is due to its excellent dynamics. The song goes from a whisper to a roar and back again several times throughout its duration, which grasps the listener's attention. For example, listen to how the song starts off quiet, gets a bit bigger during the first verse, even bigger during the B section, then comes down to just a vocal (over a gurgling synth) during the interlude, then smacks you over the head on the chorus. The same happens during the second verse, B section, interlude, and chorus, then again from the bridge to the last chorus. The tension and release is one of the main reasons the song remains interesting.

Rihanna (featuring Jay-Z)

Umbrella

Song Facts

Album: *Good Girl Gone Bad*

Writers: Jay-Z, Kuk Harrell, Terius Nash, Christopher "Tricky" Stewart

Producer: Tricky Stewart

Studio: Westlake Recording Studios (Hollywood, CA)

Release Date: March 29, 2007

Length: 4:35 (album), 4:14 (single edit)

Sales: 4.5 million worldwide

Highest Chart Position: #1 U.S. *Billboard* Hot 100, #1 U.K. Singles Chart, #1 European Hot 100, #1 in Australia, Austria, Belgium, Canada, Denmark, Germany, Hungary, Ireland, New Zealand, Norway, Romania, Slovakia, South Africa, Switzerland, and Venezuela

The lead single from her 2007 *Good Girl Gone Bad* album, "Umbrella" was a huge hit for Rihanna. The song was originally written with Britney Spears in mind, but her label rejected it.

The song was a huge success worldwide, remaining at #1 on the U.K. Singles Chart for 10 consecutive weeks (the most for the decade) and seven weeks in the U.S. One of the most played songs of the decade by radio, "Umbrella" won a Grammy for Best Rap/Sung Collaboration and was listed as #412 on *Rolling Stone*'s list of 500 Greatest Songs of All Time.

The Song

"Umbrella" once again shows how a very basic song form can be twisted slightly to make it more interesting. The album version of the song

features two different intros, while on the single version, the long rap intro is edited out. "Umbrella" also features a chorus with two distinct sections (we'll call them chorus A and B), which is highly unusual but also the hook of the song. The form looks like this:

intro A | intro B | verse | chorus A | chorus B | verse | chorus A | chorus B | bridge | chorus A | chorus B | outro (fade)

Although the melody isn't what you'd call adventurous, it's memorable and singable, something especially important for Rihanna's audience. Like many pop songs, the lyrics for "Umbrella" seem forced. Great poetry they're not, but again, that's not important when it comes to having a pop hit.

The Arrangement

As with most hit songs, the arrangement for "Umbrella" develops as it goes along, providing both movement and dynamics. The song begins with Jay-Z ad-libbing over the drums, but then goes into a second intro with a true Jay-Z rap and a Rihanna ad-lib rap against a moving synth line.

On the verse, Rihanna begins to sing the melody and Jay-Z exits. The synth line remains, but the bass synth plays only the downbeat of every chord. On the chorus, the bass synth plays whole notes (which is unusual), turning into a pad as the vocal melody changes. On the second part of the chorus, the bass synth goes back to playing just the downbeat of the chords as a second synth line enters.

On the second verse, the instrumentation is the same as the first except another synth line is added; also, to add motion to the song, the turnaround lines at the middle and end of the verse are much more active. On the A part of the second chorus, harmony vocals

Photo: Anthony Cutajar/atlasicons.com

are introduced at the ends of the phrases, while the low synth pad continues into the chorus's B section along with a new high string line.

The bridge in "Umbrella" differs from most in that instead of being the song's peak, it actually lightens the intensity by going from a doubled lead vocal to only a single, and a piano and soft string line take the place of the bass synth. The high point comes during chorus's turnaround, when all instruments play along with the strings to bring the song to its peak.

On the final chorus, yet another new string line is introduced, but the harmony vocals only occur on the very last phrase, this time as a three-part harmony instead of two as in the previous chorus. The B part of the last chorus features a new high string line, while a new lower one also enters at the end. This leads up to a new key center and chord pattern for the outro, which ends in a slow fade.

Arrangement Elements
The Foundation: Drums
The Rhythm: Synth lines in verse, string lines in chorus
The Pad: Bass synth in chorus
The Lead: Lead vocal
The Fills: String lines in last chorus

The Sound

The sound of "Umbrella" has a number of distinguishing features. First, it uses a very live-sounding drum tone; only the snare is slightly augmented with a sound effect for a bit more power. Second, the lead vocal features a prominent stereo delay, with a shorter delay on the right side and a much longer one on the left. Both are timed to the track. The vocal is also interesting in that it's very closely doubled, which you don't even notice until the bridge when the double drops out and the single vocal is very apparent.

Another unique aspect of the song is that there's no bass guitar, with that function being assumed by a fat, low synthesizer. That in itself isn't too radical—many pop hits these days replace the bass with a synth or other low-sounding instrument—but the fact that it also acts as a pad during the choruses is very uncommon, since an instrument that functions like a bass usually has more motion. It works well here though, and nothing is lost as a result.

There are a lot of great instrumental parts in "Umbrella," but they all sound like they're from the same synth; as a result, some have a tough time clearly breaking through the mix. Plus, they all have a distorted edge, which may have more to do with the way they were generated than the sonic signal path during recording or mixing.

Listen Up

To the development of the turnarounds in the second verse.

To the long stereo delay on the vocals.

To the string lines on the last chorus.

To the resolution to a different key center on the outro.

The Production

"Umbrella" was a gigantic worldwide hit and it's tough to argue with success of that magnitude. Once again, we can see that a pop hit relies on arrangement development and song dynamics as much as song form, melody, and hook. One of the best and most unique parts of the song is the second verse, which develops from the first more because of the active turnarounds than the addition of new lines or parts. This is a more or less forgotten production technique that producer Tricky Stewart has used as a signature. It just goes to show that sometimes the best production tricks are the ones that no one else is using.

Fun.

We Are Young

Song Facts

Album: *Some Nights*

Writers: Jack Antonoff, Jeffrey Bhasker, Andrew Dost, Nathaniel Ruess

Producer: Jeff Bhasker

Studios: Jungle City Studios (New York), Massive Studios (Los Angeles), The Village Recorder (Los Angeles)

Release Date: September 20, 2011

Length: 4:10 (album), 3:51 (single)

Sales: 9+ million

Highest Chart Position: #1 U.S. *Billboard* Hot 100, #1 in twelve other countries

Fun.'s "We Are Young" is a former #1 on the Billboard Hot 100 chart and also topped the Ultimate Chart. It's the first single from the band's second studio album *Some Nights.*

"We Are Young" was released to little fanfare, but received a great boost when used on the television show *Glee*, which then led to its use in a Chevrolet Super Bowl commercial. The song stayed at #1 for 6 consecutive weeks, and set a record for selling at least 300,000 downloads for seven straight weeks.

The song came together quickly after frontman Nate Ruess met Beyonce producer Jeff Bhasker. Ruess had wanted to merge hip hop beats with electronic effects and pop rock, and Bhasker immediately saw the potential in "We Are Young" and set a recording session for a few days afterwards. Singer Janelle Monae, a friend of Bhasker's, was recruited to provide the vocals in the bridge, and did so while on tour in Bristol, England.

The song was completed and released only six months later.

"We Are Young" went on to win the 2013 Grammy for Song of the Year, and was also nominated or Record of the Year and Best Pop Duo/ Group Performance.

The Song

"We Are Young" is a very unusual song in that it has two completely different feels. The song begins with one feel, then abruptly changes to another for the remainder of the tune. Other hits might have done this over the last 60 years or so, but you'll be hard pressed to remember one. The form looks like this:

intro | verse | B section | chorus (feel change) | verse |
chorus | bridge | chorus | end

As far as the lyrics, this is another song that won't win any awards (which seems to be a growing trend in pop songs). Though the chorus hook is strong, it almost seems like the verse and especially the bridge lyrics were written as an afterthought. However, the hook is the thing, and if the chorus is strong, there's the chance of a hit.

The BPM of the song is 115 for the first verse, and 95 thereafter.

Listen Up

There's only a single B section in the song and it sets up the chorus and feel change.

To the sound of the piano, with the dry piano on left side and a short reverb on the right.

To the bridge where the "na, na" backgrounds are on the left and Janelle Monae's vocal is slightly panned to the right.

The Arrangement

The arrangement is interesting because of the instruments that are subtracted rather than what's introduced along the way. The song begins with 4 bars of a floor tom beat, which leads into the verse with the lead vocal and a piano outlining the chords. Halfway through the verse the drum feel changes with the addition of a snare, and the piano arpeggiates. At the B section, the drums stop and the piano again just plays the chords.

The chorus begins a brand-new feel with the drums playing a similar feel to the intro, but with kick and snare along with a low bass synth, 8th note piano chords and doubled lead vocals. The verse continues with the doubled vocals, and a new synth pad enters. The next chorus is identical to the first.

In the bridge, a different, mellower synth bass outlines the chords, while two sets of background vocals supply the pad and the rhythm against Janelle Monae's vocals, which are then answered by the lead vocal halfway through the section.

The first half of the last chorus has a breakdown with just the drums and a organ pad. In the second half the bass synth reenters. The song ends with the same feel as the B section with just the vocal and piano.

Arrangement Elements
The Foundation: Drums, bass
The Rhythm: Piano playing eighth notes
The Pad: Synth and organ in the chorus, strings in the verse
The Lead: Vocal (doesn't singer Nate Ruess sound like Kevin Cronin of REO Speedwagon?)
The Fills: None

The Sound

This is a rather sparse-sounding song that gets pretty dense after the feel change. There's not a lot of effects layering as most musical elements have either natural room ambience or a short room reverb for a little bit of space. It's meant to be in-your-face and personal in the beginning and at the end, and that's exactly what happens.

The floor tom sound (maybe it's tympani) is huge and takes up a lot of sonic space; as a result, the bass is pretty undefined, but that's okay because it still does the job of filling out the low end of the song.

Listen Up

To the harmony vocals on the last line at the end of the choruses.

To the bridge where the "na na" backgrounds are on the left and Janelle Monáe's vocal is slightly panned to the right.

The Production

What keeps this song interesting is the use of dynamics. The song begins quietly, then gets big with the feel change on the first chorus, and basically stays that way until the last chorus when it gets much sparser, and finally ends with just the vocal and a piano. Also, the feel change really makes the song what it is, while the bridge is also different because it features a new lead vocalist, Janelle Monáe. It's not something that you expect, and you keep thinking that it will go back to the original feel in the beginning, but that never happens (it's an appoggiatura). In fact, "We Are Young" is an all-round great example of maintaining listener interest throughout the course of a song.

Tinie Tempah (featuring Eric Turner)

Written in the Stars

Song Facts

Album: *Disc-Overy*

Writers: Eshraque Mughal, Patrick Okogwu, Eric Turner, Charlie Bernardo

Producer: iSHi

Release Date: November 2010

Length: 3:28

Sales: 1+ million

Highest Chart Position: #7 U.S. *Billboard* Pop Songs, #1 U.K. Singles Chart

Tinie Tempah's "Written in the Stars" (featuring Eric Turner) is a former #1 in Britain, and was the third single from his debut album *Disc-Overy*. The track eventually made its way to the Top 10 of *Billboard's* Pop Songs chart. The song has also proved popular in commercials and promos, being used by Major League Baseball, WrestleMania XXVII, the Premier Football League, and the USA Network.

Tempah won a Brit award for Best British Breakthrough Act in 2011, and has since gone on to win various awards at MOBO, MP3 Music, Urban Music, BT Digital Music, UK Festival, and BET. *Disc-Overy* has also been nominated for the Mercury Prize and Brit Awards' Album of the Year while receiving double-platinum certification by the British Phonograph Industry association.

The Song

"Written in the Stars" features a fairly straight-ahead form with nothing much fancy about it. It looks like:

chorus | verse | chorus | interlude | verse | chorus | interlude | chorus

Two slightly different things about this song is that it begins with the chorus, and the interlude uses a vocal instead of the more usual instrumental hook.

The lyrics of the chorus (as well as the strong melody) make this song, not the rap. In fact, it's the chorus you hear in all the commercials and promos that it's used in. The rap is pedestrian boasting, but the chorus is inspired.

The BPM of the song is 91.

The Arrangement

What's cool about this song is the development, which is certainly needed for a song with a simple form. It builds and releases, builds and releases, just like most hits.

The song begins with a reverse reverb that leads into the chorus with the lead vocal and a synth playing eighth-note chords. Halfway through, a second synth enters playing a higher pad-like line.

The verse consists of Tempah's rap over what sounds like a real drum kit (or at least real drum samples) and 16th-note arpeggiated synth chords and fills every 2 bars. Halfway through the verse, the chords change to what's played in the chorus and a pad enters with the piano playing the melody that suggests the chorus at the end of every fourth bar.

Photo: Courtesy of Piotr Drabik

On the next chorus the song gets bigger with the addition of a synth bass playing whole notes and the piano doubling the melody with the vocal. An interlude follows built around the chords of the chorus that includes gang vocal answers on beat 1 of every bar.

Halfway through the next verse, the piano enters with low whole-note octaves outlining the chords, with vocals, background vocals and synths providing fills in the spaces between the vocal. The next chorus is the same as the previous except for Tempah answering the melody on the 4th and 7th bars. A longer interlude follows with an additional 4 bars that are minus the drums. The song then goes into the last chorus, which is the same as the previous except for the addition of a distorted guitar line deep in the mix. It then ends on the last phrase of the chorus with a distorted guitar with a regenerated tube echo effect.

Arrangement Elements
The Foundation: Primarily drums, or drum-like track
The Rhythm: Delayed, arpeggiated synth throughout
The Pad: Low piano octaves in the second verse, low bass synth in the chorus
The Lead: Melody vocal which is doubled by the piano in the chorus, rap
The Fills: Synth in the verse, piano in the second verse

The Sound

The sound of "Written in the Stars" isn't what could be called state-of-the-art. The vocals are a bit spitty because of the compression, and there's a hint of distortion on everything, which may have been intentional.

One of the things that's common to most hip-hop songs is the huge kick sound, and that's present here. The snare sounds like a distorted sample that has a long envelope thanks to the compression and reverb.

Listen Up

To the tape echo effect, which you can hear on the repeats of the guitar as the song fades out. You can tell it's a tape echo (or at least a simulator) by the poor frequency response and the distortion on the repeats.

To the echo on the fills in the first verse that goes from right to left.

To the piano playing the melody of the chorus in the right channel on the second

To the kick drum drop out at the beginning of bar 3 of the second verse.

The Production

The production by iSHi is excellent; you hear a lot of subtle parts that add to the development of the song as it goes along. Parts are brought in and taken away in an effort to add some tension and release, which happens between the beginning of the verses and the rest of the song. The interludes are unusual because they're vocal instead of instrumental like in most songs, which adds a nice bridge between the chorus and verse. The second interlude also adds a harmony for development.

However, the high point of the song is definitely the chorus melody, which features an appoggiatura when the melody jumps on "a million miles away" and again at the end of the phrase on "away." It's some good evidence that you only need one appoggiatura in a song to make it a hit.

Glossary

4 on the floor A drum pattern where the bass drum plays on every beat in a measure.

A-side The primary side of a 7-inch vinyl record.

B-side The secondary side of a 7-inch vinyl record.

Airplay When a song gets played on the radio.

Ambience The background noise of an environment.

Arpeggiated The notes of a chord played in quick succession.

Arrangement The way the instruments are combined in a song.

Articulation The way a note or phrase is played or sung.

Attenuator A piece of equipment that causes a decrease in level.

Automation A system that memorizes, then plays back the position of all faders and mutes on a mixing console.

Autotune A hardware device or plug-in used to adjust the pitch of a vocalist.

B section See Pre-chorus.

Bandwidth The number of frequencies that a device will pass before the signal degrades. A human can supposedly hear from 20 Hz to 20 kHz so the bandwidth of the human ear is 20 Hz to 20 kHz.

Basics See Basic tracks.

Basic tracks Recording the rhythm section for a record, which may include all the instruments of the band, but may be only the drums, depending on the project.

Bleed Acoustic spill from a sound source other than the one intended for pickup.

Bottom Bass frequencies, the lower end of the audio spectrum. See also Low end.

Bottom end See Bottom.

BPM Beats per minute. The measure of tempo.

Breakdown When an arrangement is stripped down to only one or two elements.

Bridge An interlude that connects two parts of a song, building a harmonic connection between those parts.

Build Usually a one- or two-bar section of a song where the volume builds from soft to loud.

Cadence The number of syllables in a line.

Channel In a stereo mix, the audio sent to each speaker represents a channel. There are also mix delivery formats with four, five or more channels.

Chord When two or more notes are played at once. Songs usually contain a repeating sequence of various chords called a chord progression or pattern.

Chorus (in a song) The refrain of the song following each verse, which usually contains the hook.

Chorus (electronic effect) A type of signal processor where a detuned copy is mixed with the original signal, which creates a fatter sound.

Chucks On a guitar, 8th- or 16th-note chords muted with the hand so they have a very short sustain.

Clean A signal with no distortion.

Click A metronome feed to the headphones to help the musicians play at the correct tempo.

Clip To overload and cause distortion.

Clipping When an audio signal begins to distort because a circuit in the signal path is overloaded, the top of the waveform becomes "clipped" off and begins to look square instead of rounded. This usually results in some type of distortion, which can be either soft and barely noticeable, or horribly crunchy sounding.

Competitive level A mix level that is as loud as your competitor's mix.

Compressor A signal processing device used to compress audio dynamics.

DAW Digital audio workstation. The software application and hardware that allows your computer to record and edit audio.

dB Decibel, is a unit of measurement of sound level or loudness.

Decay The time it takes for a signal to fall below audibility.

Delay A type of signal processor that produces distinct repeats (echoes) of a signal.

Direct To "go direct" means to bypass a microphone and connect the guitar, bass, or keyboard directly into a recording device.

Double To play or sing a track a second time. The inconsistencies between both tracks when played back simultaneously make the part sound bigger.

Dynamics Whether an instrument or song is played softly or loudly. Songs that vary in dynamics are found to be expressive and interesting.

Edgy A sound with an abundance of mid-range frequencies.

Effect When a sound is changed or enhanced with delay, ambience or modulation.

Element A component or ingredient of the mix.

EQ Equalizer, or to adjust the equalizers (tone controls) to affect the timbral balance of a sound.

Equalizer A tone control that can vary in sophistication from very simple to very complex. See also Parametric equalizer.

Equalization Adjustment of the frequency spectrum to even out or alter tonal imbalances.

Feel The groove of a song and how it feels to play or listen to.

Fill A short musical passage to sustain the listener's attention between melody phrases.

Flanging The process of mixing a copy of the signal back with itself, but gradually and randomly slowing the copy down to cause the sound to "whoosh" as if it were in a wind tunnel. This was originally done by holding a finger against a tape flange (the metal part that holds the tape on the reel), hence the name.

Footballs Whole notes. Long sustaining distorted guitar chords.

Four on the floor See "4 on the floor"

Groove The pulse of the song and how the instruments dynamically breathe with it. Or, the part of a vinyl record that contains the mechanical information that is transferred to electronic info by the stylus.

Guide vocal See "scratch vocal."

Hard ending An ending to a song where the music stops completely.

Harmony When a part in a song is played (or sung) by multiple instruments, each playing a different, yet related pitch, which usually sounds pleasant to the ear.

Hz An abbreviation for Hertz, the measurement of audio frequency. 1 Hz is equivalent to one cycle of a sound waveform per second. The higher the frequency of the signal, the higher the number of Hertz, and the higher the sound. Low numbers of Hertz represent low sounds.

High end The high frequency response of a device.

Hook A catchy phrase either played or sung.

Hypercompression A condition where too much compression is used and as a result leaves the song with no dynamics, making it sound lifeless.

Intonation The accuracy of tuning anywhere along the neck of a stringed instrument like a guitar or bass. Also applies to brass, woodwinds, and piano.

Iso booth Isolation booth. An isolated section of the studio designed to eliminate leakage from coming in to the booth or leaking out.

Intonation The accuracy of tuning anywhere along the neck of a stringed instrument like a guitar or bass. Also applies to brass, woodwinds, and piano.

Key When music conforms to one particular scale. If a key changes, the music then uses another scale than the original one.

kHz Kilohertz; 1 kHz = 1000 Hz.

Layered mix When the different mix elements are put into different artificial environments by using effects such as reverb and delay.

Lazy fill A drum fill that wavers behind the beat.

Leakage Sound from a distant instrument "bleeding" into a mic pointed at another instrument. Acoustic spill from a sound source other than the one intended for pickup.

Leslie A speaker cabinet primarily used with organs that features rotating speakers.

Limiter A signal-processing device used to constrict or reduce audio dynamics, reducing the loudest peaks in volume.

Loop A small audio file, usually only four or eight beats (or measures) that's edited in a way so that it can seamlessly repeat.

Low end The lower end of the audio spectrum, or bass frequencies usually below 200 Hz.

Master A final version of a recording that is destined for distribution.

Mastering The process of turning a collection of songs into a record by making them sound like they belong together in tone, volume, and timing (spacing between songs).

Mellotron A keyboard popular in the 1960s that used tapes of recorded orchestral instruments to generate its sounds.

Mid-range Middle frequencies starting from around 250 Hz up to 4000 Hz.

Mix The final balance of a recording where the individual instruments and vocals are balanced, tonally enhanced, dynamically controlled, and effects may be added.

Modulation (effect) Using a second signal to modify the first. A chorus uses a very low frequency signal to modulate the audio signal and produce the effect.

Modulation (in a song) When a song changes to a different key.

Mono Short for monaural, or single audio playback channel.

Monaural A mix that contains a single channel and usually comes from only a one speaker.

Mute To turn an instrument or voice off in a mix.

Outboard effect Hardware devices such as compressors, reverbs, and effects boxes that are not built into a console and usually reside in an equipment rack in the control room.

Outchorus A repeating chorus at the end of a song.

Out of phase The polarity of two channels (it could be the left and right channel of a stereo program) are reversed, thereby causing the center of the program (such as the vocal) to diminish in level.

Outro The section of a song after the last chorus until the end of the song.

Overdub To record along with previously recorded tracks.

Overtone The part of a sound that give it its character and uniqueness.

Pad A long sustaining note or chord.

Pan Short for panorama; indicates the left and right position of an instrument within the stereo spectrum.

Panning Moving a sound across the stereo spectrum. If a sound appears to be coming from the right or left, the majority of the volume is panned to that channel. When a sound appears to be coming from the middle, it is panned to the center, or equally to each channel.

Pedal A sustained tone.

Phase cancellation The process during which some frequencies (usually those below 100 Hz) are slowed down ever-so slightly as they pass through a device. This is usually exaggerated by excessive use of equalization and is highly undesirable.

Pitch A musical tone.

Plug-in An add-on to a computer application that adds functionality to it. EQ, modulation, and reverb are examples of DAW plug-ins.

Pocket In the "groove" (the rhythm) with the song.

Power chords Long sustaining distorted guitar chords.

Pre-chorus A section of a song between verse and chorus sections. Sometimes called a B-section. Not found in every song.

Pre-delay The time between the dry sound and the onset of reverberation. The correct setting of the pre-delay parameter can make a difference in the clarity of the mix.

Pre-production A process of familiarizing an ensemble with the songs and arrangements before recording them.

Presence Accentuated upper mid-range frequencies (anywhere from 5 kHz to 10 kHz).

Producer The musical equivalent of a movie director, the producer has the ability to craft the songs of an artist or band technically, sonically, and musically.

Production The process of overseeing and molding the sound, the arrangement, the song form, and lyrics to create the final song.

Pumping When the level of a mix increases, then decreases noticeably. Pumping is caused by the improper setting of the attack and release times on a compressor.

Punchy A description for a quality of sound that infers good reproduction of dynamics with a strong impact. The term sometimes means emphasis in the 200 Hz and 5 kHz areas.

Record A generic term for the distribution medium of a recording. Regardless of whether it's a CD, vinyl, or a digital file, it is still known as a record.

Rehearsal A practice or trial band performance.

Release The end of a sound or phrase. See also Tension and release.

Remaster To enhance the sound quality of an existing recording.

Reverb The hardware unit or plug-in that produces artificial reverberation or room ambience.

Reverberation The persistence of sound in an environment that lingers after the original sound is produced.

Rhythm section The instruments in a band that give the song its pulse, usually the bass and drums.

Roll off To attenuate either end of the frequency spectrum.

Rushed fill A drum fill that's played ahead of the beat.

Scratch vocal A temporary vocal recorded during basic tracking with the intention of replacing it later (sometimes known as a "guide vocal").

Sibilant When a vocalist singing or pronouncing a syllable that creates a "sss" or "shhh" sound that is audibly louder than other syllables.

Snare A thin drum with springs or "strainers" underneath that create a "rattling" sound.

Snare strainers The string of springs on the bottom of the snare drum.

Song form The order in which the different sections of a song are arranged.

Soundfield The direct listening area.

Stereo When a recording is mixed as two separate channels to be played through two separate speakers (right and left).

Sympathetic vibrations Vibrations, buzzes, and rattles that occur in other drums or instruments than the one that was struck.

Tempo The rate of speed that a song is played.

Tension and release Building a listener's expectations and then relaxing them, such as dissonance to harmony, or loud to soft.

Timbre Tonal color.

Timed delay A delay where the repeats are timed to pulse along with the pulse of the song.

Top end See High end.

Track A term sometimes used to mean a song. In recording, a separate musical performance that is recorded.

Transient A very short duration signal.

Tremolo A cyclic variation in volume.

Turnaround A short transition part, usually at the end of song sections such as between a verse and chorus.

Vibe The emotional atmosphere communicated to and felt by others.

Vibrato A cyclic variation in tone.

Vocoder A type of synthesizer that uses the human voice as an oscillator.

Voicing The way the notes of a chord are distributed.

Bobby Owsinski Bibliography

The Mixing Engineer's Handbook 2nd edition (Thomson Course Technology)

The premier book on audio mixing techniques provides all the information needed to take your mixing skills to the next level. Includes advice from some of the world's best mixing engineers.

The Recording Engineer's Handbook 2nd Edition (Course Technology PTR)

This book reveals the microphone and recording techniques used by some of the most renowned recording engineers, including everything you need to know to lay down great tracks in any recording situation, in any musical genre, and in any studio.

The Audio Mastering Handbook 2nd Edition (Course Technology PTR)

Everything you always wanted to know about mastering, from doing it yourself to using a major facility, utilizing insights from some of the world's top mastering engineers.

The Drum Recording Handbook with DVD (with Dennis Moody) (Hal Leonard)

Uncovers the secret of amazing drum recordings in your recording, even with the most inexpensive gear. It's all in the technique, and this book & DVD will show you how.

How To Make Your Band Sound Great with DVD (Hal Leonard)

This band improvement book and DVD shows your band how to play to its fullest potential: how to be tight, more dynamic, and how to improve your live show and recordings.

The Studio Musician's Handbook with DVD (with Paul ILL) (Hal Leonard)

Everything you wanted to know about the world of the studio musician including how you become a studio musician, who hires you, how much you get paid, what kind of skills you need, what gear you must have, the proper session etiquette required to make a session run smoothly, and how to apply these skills in every type of recording session.

Music 3.0 - A Survival Guide To Making Music In The Internet Age 2nd Edition (Hal Leonard)

The paradigm has shifted and everything you knew about the music business has completely changed. Who are the new players in the music business? Why are traditional record labels, television, and radio no longer factors in an artist's success? How do you market and distribute your music in the new music world—and how do you make money? This book answers these questions and more in its comprehensive look at the new music business.

The Music Producer's Handbook with DVD (Hal Leonard)
Reveals the secrets to becoming a music producer and producing just about any kind of project in any genre of music. The book also covers the true mechanics of production, from analyzing and fixing the format of a song to troubleshooting a song when it just doesn't sound right, to getting the best performance and sound out of the band and vocalist.

The Musician's Video Handbook with DVD (Hal Leonard)
A musician's guide to making any of the various types of videos now required by a musical artist for promotion or final product. The book explains tricks and tips used by the pros to make their videos look professional, which you can do with inexpensive gear and not much of a budget.

Mixing And Mastering With IK Multimedia T-RackS: The Official Guide (Course Technology PTR)
Learn how to harness the potential of T-RackS and learn the tips and tricks of using T-RackS processor modules to help bring your mixes to life, then master them so they're competitive with any major label release.

The Touring Musician's Handbook with DVD (Hal Leonard)
This handbook covers all you need to know as a touring musician, whether you're a sideman, solo performer, or member of a band. As a bonus, individual touring guides for guitarists, bassists, drummers, vocalists, keyboard players, horn players, and string players as well as interviews with famous and influential touring musicians are included.

The Ultimate Guitar Tone Handbook with DVD (with Rich Tozolli) (Alfred Music)
The Ultimate Guitar Tone Handbook is the definitive book for discovering that great guitar sound and making sure it records well. The book definitively outlines all the factors that make electric and acoustic guitars, and amplifiers and speaker cabinets sound the way they do, as well as the classic and modern recording and production techniques that capture great tone. *The Ultimate Guitar Tone Handbook* also features a series of interviews with expert players, technicians, recording engineers, producers and manufacturers that gives you an inside look into the business of guitar tone, and an accompanying DVD provides both an audio and visual reference point for achieving the classic sounds you hear on records.

The Studio Builder's Handbook with DVD (with Dennis Moody) (Alfred Music)
No matter how good your recording gear is, chances are you're not getting the best possible sound because of the deficiencies of your room. While you might think that it costs thousands of dollars and the services of an acoustic designer to improve your studio, the *Studio Builder's Handbook* will strip away the mystery of what makes a